THE JUNGLE

Upton Sinclair

SPARK PUBLISHING

SPARKNOTES is a registered trademark of SparkNotes LLC

Spark Publishing
A Division of Barnes & Noble
120 Fifth Avenue
New York, NY 10011
www.sparknotes.com

ISBN-13: 978-1-4114-0378-9
ISBN-10: 1-4114-0378-9

Please submit changes or report errors to www.sparknotes.com/errors.

Printed in the United States.

10 9 8 7 6 5 4 3 2 1

CONTENTS

Context

UPTON SINCLAIR WAS BORN on September 20, 1878, in Baltimore, Maryland. His family had once belonged to the southern aristocracy but, at Sinclair's birth, the family hovered near poverty. Sinclair graduated from high school early and enrolled in the City College of New York at the age of fourteen. When he was fifteen, he began writing to support himself and help pay his college expenses. During his college years, Sinclair encountered socialist philosophy, the influence of which is evident in his writing throughout his life, and became an avid supporter of the Socialist Party. After he graduated from college, he enrolled in Columbia University as a graduate student in 1897.

Sinclair published five novels between 1901 and 1906, but none of them generated much income. Late in 1904, the editors of the popular socialist newspaper *Appeal to Reason* sent Sinclair to Chicago to examine the lives of stockyard workers. He spent seven weeks in the city's meatpacking plants, learning every detail about the work itself, the home lives of workers, and the structure of the business. *The Jungle* was born from this research and was first published in serial form in *Appeal to Reason*. The first few publishers whom Sinclair approached told him that his novel was too shocking, and he financed a first publication of the book himself. Eventually, however, Sinclair did find a willing commercial publisher, and in 1906, *The Jungle* was published in its entirety.

With the instant success of *The Jungle,* Sinclair took his place in the ranks of the "muckrakers," a term that Theodore Roosevelt coined in 1906 to refer to a group of journalists who devoted themselves to exposing the ills of industrialization. *The Jungle* raised a public outcry against the unhealthy standards in the meatpacking industry and provoked the passage of The Pure Food and Drug Act of 1906. No novel since Harriet Beecher Stowe's *Uncle Tom's Cabin,* first published in 1851, had made such a social impact. The novel's success satisfied Sinclair's financial concerns but not his political motivations for writing it. Sinclair had intended the novel to elicit sympathy for the working class and build support for the Socialist movement. His readership, however, was more moved by the threat of tainted beef than the plight of the worker. Sinclair tried to translate the success of *The Jungle* into large-scale social change by building a utopian colony in New Jersey with the profits from the novel, but the colony burned down four months after its inception.

In 1911, Sinclair divorced his first wife and married Mary Craig Kimbrough, a writer. They moved to California, where Sinclair continued to write in support of socialism. During the Great Depression, Sinclair organized the End Poverty in California movement. In 1934, he ran as a democrat in an unsuccessful campaign to become California's governor. During the 1940s, he returned to writing fiction. He enjoyed a revival in popularity and won a Pulitzer Prize for *Dragon's Teeth*, a novel dealing with Nazism in Germany.

Sinclair and his wife moved to a small town in Arizona in the 1950s. After Kimbrough died in 1961, Sinclair married again. His third wife died in 1967, and Sinclair died in 1968. Though he published more than eighty books after *The Jungle,* he is most remembered for this novel. In the aftermath of the Soviet Union, the Warsaw Pact, and the Berlin Wall, the novel's idealistic glorification of socialism may seem naïve, but the novel remains an important social record of the psychology of American capitalism in the early twentieth century.

Plot Overview

J URGIS RUDKUS AND ONA LUKOSZAITE, a young man and woman who have recently immigrated to Chicago from Lithuania, hold their wedding feast at a bar in an area of Chicago known as Packingtown. The couple and several relatives have come to Chicago in search of a better life, but Packingtown, the center of Lithuanian immigration and of Chicago's meatpacking industry, is a hard, dangerous, and filthy place where it is difficult to find a job. After the reception, Jurgis and Ona discover that they are more than a hundred dollars in debt to the saloonkeeper. In Lithuania, custom dictates that guests at a wedding-feast leave money to cover the cost, but in America, many of the impoverished immigrants depart from the feast without leaving any money. Jurgis, who has great faith in the American Dream, vows that he will simply work harder to make more money.

Jurgis, who is young and energetic, quickly finds work, as do Marija Berczynskas, Ona's cousin, and Jonas, the brother of Ona's stepmother, Teta Elzbieta. The family signs an agreement to buy a house, but it turns out to be a swindle; the agreement is full of hidden costs, and the house is shoddy and poorly maintained. As the family's living expenses increase, even Ona and young Stanislovas, one of Teta Elzbieta's children, are forced to look for jobs. Jobs in Packingtown involve back-breaking labor, however, conducted in unsafe conditions with little regard for individual workers. Furthermore, the immigrant community is fraught with crime and corruption. Jurgis's father, Dede Antanas, finds a job only after agreeing to pay another man a third of his wages for helping him obtain the job. But the job is too difficult for the old man, and it quickly kills him.

Winter is the most dangerous season in Packingtown and even Jurgis, forced to work in an unheated slaughterhouse in which it is difficult to see, risks his life every day by simply going to work. Marija is courted by Tamoszius, a likable violinist, but the couple is never able to marry because they never have enough money to hold a wedding. Marija's factory closes down and she loses her job. Distressed about the terrible conditions of his family members' lives, Jurgis joins a union and slowly begins to understand the web of political corruption and bribery that makes Packingtown run. Hoping to improve his lot, Jurgis begins trying to learn English. Marija regains her job, but she is fired when she complains about being cheated out of some of her pay. Ona is now pregnant, and her job has become increasingly difficult for her. Her supervisor, Miss Henderson, oversees a prostitution ring, and most of the other girls at the factory are made to be prostitutes. Ona gives birth to a healthy boy, whom she and Jurgis name Antanas after Jurgis's late father, but she is forced to return to work only seven days later.

In Packingtown, any mishap can bring ruin upon a family. Jurgis sprains his ankle and is forced to spend nearly three months in bed, unable to work. Even though poor working conditions caused the accident, the factory simply cuts off Jurgis's pay while he recuperates. Unable to tolerate the misery, Jonas abandons the family, disappearing without a word. Kristoforas, the youngest son of Teta Elzbieta, dies of food poisoning. Jurgis at last recovers and returns to work, but the factory refuses to give him his job back. After a long, frustrating search for employment, Jurgis is forced to take a job at the fertilizer plant, the foulest place in all of Packingtown. He begins to numb himself with alcohol.

Ona is pregnant again. One night, she doesn't return home from work, and Jurgis discovers that Phil Connor, her boss, kept her after work and forced her to sleep with him. Jurgis attacks Connor and is arrested. After an unfair trial, Jurgis is sentenced to a month in prison; the family will again be forced to scrape by without his wages. In prison, Jurgis befriends a criminal named Jack Duane. When he is released, Jurgis discovers that his family has been evicted from its home and is living at the run-down boardinghouse in which they first stayed when they arrived in Chicago. When he enters the boardinghouse, he finds Ona screaming; she is prematurely in labor, and the effort of giving birth kills her and the child. In agony, Jurgis disappears on a drinking binge.

At last, Teta Elzbieta convinces Jurgis to think of his son, and he again begins searching for a job. Through the philanthropy of a wealthy woman who takes an interest in the family, Jurgis finds a good job at a steel mill. He dedicates himself to Antanas and feels renewed hope in life. But his hopes are shattered when Antanas drowns in the mud-logged street. In despair, Jurgis abandons his surviving family members and wanders the countryside as a tramp.

In the winter, Jurgis returns to Chicago, where he finds a job digging freight tunnels. After injuring himself at work, he is forced to spend some time in the hospital. When he is released, he has no money and cannot find work, so he becomes a beggar. One night, a wealthy young man named Freddie Jones gives him a one-hundred-dollar bill, but when Jurgis asks a bartender to change it for him, the man cheats him, giving him ninety-five cents back. Jurgis attacks the man and is again sent to jail. In prison, he meets Jack Duane again. When the two men are released, Jurgis becomes Duane's partner, and the two commit burglaries and muggings. Jurgis is eventually recruited to work for the corrupt political boss, Mike Scully. When a series of strikes hits Packingtown, Jurgis crosses the picket lines, undermining the efforts of the union but making a great deal of money as a scab.

One day, Jurgis sees Phil Connor again and attacks him. He is again sent to prison and, because Connor is a crony of Mike Scully, Jurgis's meager political connections do not help him. After being released, he is forced to live on charity. By this time, Jurgis has completely lost touch with his family. One day, however, he meets an old acquaintance who tells him how to find Marija. He learns that Marija has become a prostitute to help support Teta Elzbieta and the children. She is also addicted to morphine. Jurgis wants to see Teta Elzbieta again but not until he finds a good job.

One night, his spirit all but crushed by privation and misery, Jurgis wanders into a socialist political rally, in which an orator delivers a speech that fills Jurgis with inspiration. Jurgis joins the socialist party and embraces its ideal that the workers—not a few wealthy capitalists—should own factories and plants. Jurgis finds a job as a porter at a socialist-run hotel and is reunited with Teta Elzbieta. He attends a socialist rally in which the speaker sums up Jurgis's new beliefs: if more people convert to socialism, the speaker declares, then "Chicago will be ours!"

CHARACTER LIST

Jurgis Rudkus A Lithuanian immigrant who comes to America with his wife, Ona. Jurgis is a strong, determined individual with a faith in the American Dream of self-betterment, but his health, family, and hopes are slowly destroyed by the miserable working and living conditions in Packingtown. Jurgis, who doesn't elicit much more from the reader than pity, is an obvious instrument that Sinclair uses to express his vision of the exploitation of the worker by capitalism and his redemption by socialism.

Ona Lukoszaite Teta Elzbieta's stepdaughter and Jurgis's wife. A kind, lovely, and optimistic girl, Ona is ruined by the forces of capitalism that work against the family, particularly after she is raped by her boss, Phil Connor.

Teta Elzbieta Lukoszaite Ona's stepmother and the mother of six others. A resilient, strong-willed old woman, Teta Elzbieta is one of the strongest and most important characters in *The Jungle*. Sinclair uses her to represent the redemptive power of family, home, and tradition.

Marija Berczynskas Ona's cousin, who travels to America with the rest of the family because her employer in the old country is unkind to her. Marija is a large, strong woman, capable of standing up for herself; because she first tries to fight back against the corrupt bosses, she represents a spirit of defiance among the immigrants that is slowly crushed.

Phil Connor Ona's boss, who sexually harasses her at the factory where she works. A bullying, depraved man, Connor represents the moral corruption of power in Chicago as well as the complicated relationship between politics, crime, and business. He has ties to all three and, thus, has the power to destroy Jurgis's life.

Dede Antanas Rudku Jurgis's father, who travels to America with the rest of the family. A proud man, Dede Antanas is prevented by his old age from obtaining a job through normal means. He has to resort to the humiliation of paying a man a third of his wages in return for a job, whose unsanitary and unsafe working conditions destroy his health.

Antanas Rudkus Ona and Jurgis's son. Antanas is a strong, sturdy little boy, but he drowns in the mud in the street while Jurgis is at work. The death of Antanas signals the death of hope in Jurgis's life.

Grandmother Majauszkiene The family's Lithuanian neighbor when they move into their house. A concerned old woman, Grandmother Majauszkiene has lived in Packingtown for many years and has seen one generation after another of immigrants ground into ruin by the merciless labor practices of the factories. She became a socialist before she even came to America.

Juozapas Lukoszaite One of Teta Elzbieta's two crippled children, injured when a wagon ran over one of his legs when he was a toddler. Juozapas unwittingly helps the family when he meets a rich lady while foraging for food in the local dump.

Kotrina Lukoszaite One of Teta Elzbieta's children, who is forced to care for the children and do household chores. When Jurgis is sent to prison, Kotrina has to go to work selling newspapers on the streets with her able-bodied brothers.

Stanislovas Lukoszaite One of Teta Elzbieta's children, a young boy of about fourteen. Stanislovas shirks his responsibilities as a wage earner because he is terrified of frostbite. Jurgis often has to beat him to make him go to work.

Jonas   Teta Elzbieta's brother, who first encourages the family to travel to America. After months of poverty in Packingtown, Jonas disappears, and the family never hears from him again. His absence deprives the family of a key wage earner and throws them into a greater financial crisis.

Jack Duane A polished, charismatic criminal whom Jurgis meets during his first prison term. Jack later introduces Jurgis to Chicago's criminal underworld, where money comes easily to Jurgis for the first time in America.

Miss Henderson The forelady in Ona's factory. Cruel and bitter, Miss Henderson is the jilted mistress of one of the factory superintendents. She also runs a brothel and arranges to get jobs for some of the prostitutes who work for her. She hates Ona because Ona is a "decent married girl," and she and her toadies try to make Ona as miserable as possible.

Tommy Hinds The proprietor of a small Chicago hotel and a well-known proponent of socialism. Jurgis obtains a job as Hinds's porter not long after his conversion to socialism.

Ostrinski A Polish immigrant who speaks Lithuanian. After Jurgis hears a rousing speech at a socialist political meeting, Ostrinski is assigned the task of teaching Jurgis about socialism.

Nicholas Schliemann A spokesperson for socialism. Nicholas gives a long explanation of socialist philosophy to a magazine editor who has written against socialism in the past. He functions as a mouthpiece for Sinclair's own political philosophy.

Mike Scully A corrupt, wealthy democrat in Chicago who owns the festering dump in which Juozapas and other children forage for food. Scully makes money off the housing scheme to which Jurgis's family falls victim.

He works at rigging elections, and Jurgis becomes one of his henchmen during his brief stint in the Chicago criminal underworld.

Jokubas Szedvilas The failing proprietor of a delicatessen in Packingtown who knows Jonas from the old country. A kind but troubled man, Jokubas represents the harsh reality of capitalism and reveals the naïveté of Jurgis's dreams of success.

ANALYSIS OF MAJOR CHARACTERS

JURGIS

Throughout *The Jungle*, Sinclair's characters are not so much well-rounded, believable characters as they are representative figures of the immigrant working class as a whole. The greatest evidence of Sinclair's use of Jurgis to garner sympathy and admiration is that he doesn't possess any true character flaw. When he acts immorally or selfishly, as when he goes out drinking after Ona's death or abandons the family after Antanas's death, we are always meant to understand that he does so out of the hurt and misery that his environment forces upon him. Jurgis's characteristics are designed to make him appealing to the average American reader of 1906, and at the beginning of the novel, he has no unsympathetic traits. He is young, strong, optimistic, energetic, devoted to his family, and enthusiastic about his new country. He has a powerful belief in the American Dream—the idea that hard work will beget rewards. When Ona worries about the debt that their wedding feast will force them to assume, Jurgis earnestly promises, "I will work harder," as though doing so will guarantee material success.

As Jurgis's idealism and naïveté are slowly ground into oblivion by the oppressive conditions of life in Packingtown, the pain causes Jurgis to act out of character for long periods of time. The values with which he first equips himself in his pursuit of happiness begin to seem irrelevant: he uses his earnings to drink heavily instead of saving, he abandons his family, and he turns to corruption and crime as a source of income. But at no point are we meant to judge Jurgis harshly or think that he is simply an immoral, uncaring person. On the contrary, we are supposed to bear in mind that he is the exact *opposite* sort of person. Jurgis presents an idealized portrait of the working poor; his degradation illustrates how capitalism fails the working class.

ONA LUKOSZAITE

Like Jurgis, Ona is more a type than an individual, and Sinclair constructs her as an appealing feminine contrast to Jurgis's masculinity. Whereas Jurgis is confident and optimistic, Ona is fragile and easily frightened, as when she frets over the cost of the wedding feast mere moments after marrying Jurgis. Ona is extremely young—not even sixteen at the start of the novel—and is presented as a delicate, lovely picture of female traits that Sinclair believed his readers would find laudable: docility, loyalty, and trust in her husband and family. Ona experiences a crisis when Phil Connor rapes her, and she takes on a more independent existence when she lies to Jurgis about her whereabouts so that he will not guess what has happened to her. But generally, throughout the novel, Ona is mainly portrayed as a girl for Jurgis to love and a wife to complete the family ideal that Sinclair repeatedly exposes to the destructive forces of capitalism. Ona's death occurs in Chapter 19, only slightly more than halfway through the novel, and her final months are largely a slide into increased fragility and poor health caused by her return to work only a week after giving birth to Antanas. In this way, Ona's death is portrayed as another sacrifice that Jurgis must make to capitalism, which pulls his family apart before he can even fully establish it.

Teta Elzbieta Lukoszaite

In contrast to Jurgis and her stepdaughter Ona, Teta Elzbieta is not young; she is a mother of six living children and is nearing old age at the start of the novel. Where Jurgis has energy, Teta Elzbieta has inner strength; where he has faith in his work ethic, she has a commitment to her home and family. Throughout the novel, she represents the strength of family and traditions of the old country. For this reason, as the novel progresses, Teta Elzbieta gradually emerges as one of its strongest and most important characters. Forced to endure innumerable privations, from the disappearance of her brother Jonas to the deaths of two of her own children and her stepdaughter Ona, Teta Elzbieta remains steady and strong. She is willing to work when the family needs her to, but her real place is in the home, and her transition into the world outside it represents another powerful blow to the family. At the end of the novel, however, she has quietly weathered the worst of the storm and is able to survive with the fragments of her family around her. Pragmatic rather than stubborn, she accepts Jurgis back into the family after his long abandonment because he can provide for the family. Her experiences dealing with adversity have molded her outlook such that she judges Jurgis and his new socialist politics based on his and their immediate benefit to the family.

THEMES, MOTIFS & SYMBOLS

THEMES

Themes are the fundamental and often universal ideas explored in a literary work.

SOCIALISM AS A REMEDY FOR THE EVILS OF CAPITALISM

The main theme of *The Jungle* is the evil of capitalism. Every event, especially in the first twenty-seven chapters of the book, is chosen deliberately to portray a particular failure of capitalism, which is, in Sinclair's view, inhuman, destructive, unjust, brutal, and violent. The slow annihilation of Jurgis's immigrant family at the hands of a cruel and prejudiced economic and social system demonstrates the effect of capitalism on the working class as a whole. As the immigrants, who initially possess an idealistic faith in the American Dream of hard work leading to material success, are slowly used up, tortured, and destroyed, the novel relentlessly illustrates that capitalism is to blame for their plight and emphasizes that the characters' individual stories are the stories of millions of people. *The Jungle* is not a thematically nuanced or complicated novel: capitalism is simply portrayed as a total evil, from its greedy destruction of children to its cynical willingness to sell diseased meat to an unsuspecting public. Sinclair opts not to explore the psychology of capitalism; instead, he simply presents a long litany of the ugly effects of capitalism on the world.

In Sinclair's view, socialism is the cure for all of the problems that capitalism creates. When Jurgis discovers socialist politics in Chapter 28, it becomes clear that the novel's attack on capitalism is meant to persuade the reader of the desirability of the socialist alternative. When socialism is introduced, it is shown to be as good as capitalism is evil; whereas capitalism destroys the many for the benefit of the few, socialism works for the benefit of everyone. It is even speculated that a socialist state could fulfill Christian morality. Again, there is no nuance in the book's polemic: *The Jungle*'s goal is to persuade the reader to adopt socialism. Every aspect of the novel's plot, characterization, and conflict is designed to discredit the capitalist political system and illustrate the ability of a socialist political system to restore humanity to the downtrodden, exploited, and abused working class.

THE IMMIGRANT EXPERIENCE AND THE HOLLOWNESS OF THE AMERICAN DREAM

Because the family that Sinclair uses to represent the struggle of the working class under capitalism is a group of Lithuanian immigrants, the novel is also able to explore the plight of immigrants in America. Jurgis, Teta Elzbieta, and their family come to America based on the promise of high wages and a happy, good life. From the outset, they maintain an unshakable faith in the American Dream—the idea that hard work and morality will yield material success and happiness. But Sinclair exposes the hypocrisy of the American Dream as the family members attempt to plug themselves into this naïve equation: virtually every aspect of the family's experience in Packingtown runs counter to the myth of America to which they subscribe. Instead of a land of acceptance and opportunity, they find a place of prejudice and exploitation; instead of a country where hard work and morality lead to success, they find a place where only moral corruption, crime, and graft enable one to succeed materially.

Because he wants his readers to sympathize with Jurgis, Sinclair goes to great lengths to ensure that this immigrant family doesn't seem alien or foreign to the American mind. He repeatedly emphasizes that their values of hard work, family togetherness, honesty, and thrift are those of the American reading public. Sinclair doesn't attack the American Dream; instead, he uses the disintegration of the family to illustrate his belief that capitalism itself is an attack on the values that support the American Dream, which has long since been rendered hollow by the immoral value of greed.

MOTIFS

Motifs are recurring structures, contrasts, and literary devices that can help to develop and inform the text's major themes.

CORRUPTION

As Jurgis and his family members experience harder and harder times in Packingtown, they find themselves surrounded increasingly with signs of immorality and corruption—laws that are not enforced, politicians out for their own gain, salesmen who lie about their wares—a whole community of people trying desperately to get ahead by taking advantage of one another. At the beginning of the novel, the signs of corruption are slight; a few people neglect to leave money to pay for the wedding feast. By the end of the novel, however, Jurgis has been a thief, mugger, strikebreaker, and an agent in a political vote-buying scheme. The family itself has been subject to swindles, grafts, manipulation, and rape. As the corruption motif recurs with increasing levels of immorality, it enhances the sense that things are growing worse and worse for the family. Sinclair heightens the atmosphere of grim tragedy and hopelessness to such an extent that only the encounter with socialism in Chapter 28 can possibly alleviate Jurgis's suffering and give his life meaning.

FAMILY AND TRADITION

Counterbalancing the motif of human corruption and depravity in the novel is the positive portrayal of the essential goodness of family and social traditions such as the wedding feast in Chapter 1. One of the novel's central criticisms of capitalism is that it has a destructive effect on the family. For Jurgis's family, economic hardship at various times helps disintegrate the family: Jonas disappears, Jurgis abandons the family, and Marija becomes a morphine-addicted prostitute. As the novel progresses, the role of family diminishes as the individual characters become increasingly battered and beaten: when Kristoforas dies, for instance, Jurgis is relieved because it means one less mouth to feed in the house. But because of the strength of Teta Elzbieta, the character who most directly represents the home and family, the clan is never quite destroyed. After Jurgis's reunion with Teta Elzbieta at the end of the novel, not long after his discovery of socialism, the book even brings a measure of optimism into its portrayal of the family's future, as Teta Elzbieta welcomes his earning power back into the family.

SYMBOLS

Symbols are objects, characters, figures, and colors used to represent abstract ideas or concepts.

PACKINGTOWN AND THE STOCKYARDS

Perhaps the novel's most important symbol is the animal pens and slaughterhouses of Packingtown, which represent in a simple, direct way the plight of the working class. Just as the animals at Packingtown are herded into pens, killed with impunity, made to suffer, and given no choice about their fate, so too are the thousands of poor immigrant workers forced to enter the machinery of capitalism, which grinds them down and kills them without giving them any choice. Waves of animals pass through Packingtown in a constant flow, as thousands of them are slaughtered every day and replaced by more, just as generations of immigrants are ruined by the merciless work and the oppression of capitalism and eventually replaced by new generations of immigrants.

CANS OF ROTTEN MEAT
Historically, *The Jungle*'s most important effect was probably the passage of the Pure Food and Drug Act of 1906, enacted in response to public outcry over the novel's portrayal of the meat industry's practice of selling rotten and diseased meat to unsuspecting customers. Sinclair uses the cans of rotten and unhealthy meat to represent the essential corruption of capitalism and the hypocrisy of the American Dream. The cans have shiny, attractive surfaces but contain a mass of putrid meat unfit for human consumption. In the same way, American capitalism presents an attractive face to immigrants, but the America that they find is rotten and corrupt.

THE JUNGLE
The novel's title symbolizes the competitive nature of capitalism; the world of Packingtown is like a Darwinian jungle, in which the strong prey on the weak and all living things are engaged in a brutal, amoral fight for survival. The title of the novel draws attention specifically to the doctrine of Social Darwinism, an idea used by some nineteenth-century thinkers to justify the abuses of wealthy capitalists. This idea essentially held that society was designed to reward the strongest, best people, while inferior people were kept down at a suitable level. By relating the story of a group of honest, hardworking immigrants who are destroyed by corruption and evil, Sinclair tries to rebut the idea of Social Darwinism, implying that those who succeed in the capitalist system are not the best of humankind but rather the worst and most corrupt of all.

Summary & Analysis

Chapters 1–2

Summary: Chapter 1

Around the turn of the twentieth century, Ona Lukoszaite and Jurgis Rudkus, two Lithuanian immigrants who have recently arrived in Chicago, are being married. They hold their *veselija,* or wedding feast, according to Lithuanian custom. The celebration takes place in a hall near the Chicago stockyards in an area of the city known as Packingtown because it is the center of the meat-packing industry. Food, beer, and music fill the hall. Following Lithuanian tradition, hungry people lingering in the doorway are invited inside to eat their fill. The musicians play badly but, amid the general festivity, no one seems to mind.

The highlight of the celebration is the *acziavimas:* the guests, linking their hands, form a rotating circle while the musicians play; the bride stands in the middle and each male guest takes a turn dancing with her. After the dance, each male guest is expected to drop money into a hat, held by Teta Elzbieta, Ona's stepmother. Each gives according to his means, helping the newlyweds pay for the *veselija,* which can cost upward of three hundred dollars—more than a year's wages for many of the guests.

Many unscrupulous guests take advantage of the families of the newlyweds at these celebrations, however, filling themselves with food and drink and leaving without contributing any money. Some leave with open contempt while others sneak away. Often, the saloon-keeper cheats families on the beer and liquor, claiming that the guests consumed more than they actually did. Often, they serve the worst swill they have after the families have bargained for a certain quality of alcohol at a fixed price. The immigrants quickly learn not to antagonize these barmen because they are often connected with powerful district politicians. The honest guests and friends of the newlyweds bear the greater burden of the cost owing to the predators who attend.

Noticing that many people are leaving without paying, Ona becomes frightened and worried about the cost of the ceremony, but Jurgis promises that they will find some way to pay the bill. He vows that he will simply work harder and earn more money. The celebration is overshadowed by the knowledge that most of the men who are lucky enough to have jobs must report to work early in the morning. If a worker is one minute late, he loses an hour's pay; if he is twenty minutes late, he loses his job. Getting fired means waiting for hours in doorways for up to weeks at a time to obtain another job. In Packingtown, men, women, and children alike work grueling hours for the most paltry of wages.

SUMMARY: CHAPTER 2

The narrator sketches background information about Jurgis and his family. Young and powerfully built, Jurgis came to Chicago from the rural countryside of Lithuania. In Lithuania, Ona's father died, leaving his family troubled by debt. They lost their farm and had little in cash savings. They spoke of traveling to America, where the wages were much higher. Ona did not want to leave her siblings or Teta Elzbieta behind. Teta Elzbieta's brother Jonas knew of a man who made a fortune in America, inspiring the family to work to make the trip possible. Jurgis worked for months to save money to help pay for the cost of the voyage. His father, Dede Antanas, resolved to go with his son and Ona's family. Marija Berczynskas, Ona's cousin, joined the family after suffering the abuse of an unkind employer in her homeland. She reckoned that her powerful physique would earn her more money and respect in America. Jurgis and his extended family, twelve in all, fell prey to various con artists in Lithuania and America. By the time they reached Chicago after landing in New York, their store of savings had dwindled.

By a stroke of luck, Jonas spies the delicatessen of Jokubas Szedvilas, the Lithuanian man whom he claimed had made a fortune. Jokubas owns a delicatessen in Chicago but, rather than living like a king, he is suffering financial troubles. He directs Jonas and the family to a miserable, overcrowded boardinghouse run by an impoverished widow, where they take up residence. Jurgis and Ona go for a walk through their new neighborhood. The stench of rotting animal flesh and animal excrement, along with billowing smoke, fills the air. Children pick through the nearby garbage dump. Much of the land surrounding the stockyards is "made land," or filled dumps where buildings have now been constructed. After gazing at Packingtown in the distance for a few moments, Jurgis promises to "go there and get a job!"

Analysis: Chapters 1 and 2

Sinclair employs a spare, journalistic style that tries to convey an exacting realism, which had a precedent in American fiction in novelists such as Theodore Dreiser, who wrote about the social problems of industrialization, and Stephen Crane, who grimly portrayed the horrors of the Civil War in *The Red Badge of Courage*. But while these earlier authors' realism had a more literary pedigree, Sinclair's realism comes from journalism—muckraking journalism, which exposes misconduct on the part of an individual or business, in particular. Sinclair splatters the page with a surfeit of details that are intended not so much to create atmosphere as to drive home a message. The facts presented are never neutral or ambiguous. Sinclair's occasional use of the second person ("to spend such a sum, all in a single day of your life") heightens the reader's sense of experiencing the life that Sinclair describes in full, gritty detail.

During the period of industrialization at the end of the nineteenth century and beginning of the twentieth, the millions of poor immigrants that flocked to the United States met with terrible working conditions and barely livable wages. Moreover, they encountered hostility and racism from the citizens of their new homeland. Their unfamiliar cultural practices were regarded as a threat to traditional American culture. To build a case for socialism, Sinclair had to persuade the American reading public to sympathize with the very people whom many regarded with suspicion and hostility. In the opening chapters, Sinclair endeavors to reduce the alien character of the Lithuanian immigrant family that occupies the center of his narrative by showing them in an extremely sympathetic setting—a wedding feast. Nevertheless, he doesn't pretend to portray them as entirely assimilated to American culture, since doing so would diminish their cultural heritage. Rather, of course, the wedding feast is held according to Lithuanian tradition. In this way, though the novel opens with the Lithuanian custom of the *veselija,* Sinclair emphasizes that the immigrants share a great many social values with the American reading public. The central values expressed in the *veselija* are family, community, and charity: according to custom, the community charitably shares in the expense of the celebration and donates money to help the new couple start out in life. The celebration is an expression of commitment to community and tradition as well as to the institution of marriage.

Just as Sinclair wishes to inspire sympathy for the immigrant family by getting his readers to identify with their social values, so too does he attempt to sway opinion against the unwholesome social values that menace the immigrants. The young con artists and the corrupt saloonkeepers, who represent dishonesty and thievery, respectively, have assimilated the brutal, predatory values of consumer capitalism. They value their personal gain above the social values of family, community, and charity. Hence, Sinclair identifies capitalism as hostile to American moral values; in this way, the opening chapters of the novel immediately begin to build a case for socialism.

Moreover, Jurgis and Ona's family immigrates to America in search of the American Dream, the advertisement by which America sells itself as the land of freedom and opportunity. This myth, represented in Chapter 2 by the character of Jokubas, promises them that hard work and commitment to social values will win them success. But Sinclair immediately begins to portray this dream of America as a naïve fantasy: Jokubas is a struggling delicatessen operator, not a thriving capitalist. Furthermore, from the moment the immigrants arrive in the country they fall prey to various greedy individuals who profit unfairly from their ignorance. Sinclair means to depict these events as a betrayal of the very values upon which the American identity is based. Jurgis's response to the con artists taking advantage of the *veselija* is "I will work harder." Again, Sinclair wishes to identify the immigrant laborer with the values of the American reading public. Jurgis calmly faces adversity and expresses a profound belief in the ethic of work, a fundamental American value.

CHAPTERS 3–5

SUMMARY: CHAPTER 3

Jokubas takes the family on a tour of Packingtown. They are amazed to see pens packed with tens of thousands of cattle, pigs, and sheep. The suffering of the animals, which will all be killed by the end of the day, daunts even Jurgis's optimism. But the flurry of human activity fills Jurgis with wonder. Jokubas notes sarcastically the signs regarding the sanitation rules. The government inspector who checks the slaughtered pigs for signs of tuberculosis often lets several carcasses go unchecked. Spoiled meat is specially doctored in secret before it is scattered among the rest of the meat in preparation for canning and packing.

Summary: Chapter 4

Jurgis begins his job of sweeping the entrails of slaughtered cattle through trap doors. Despite the stench, he is filled with optimism because he earns a little over two dollars for twelve hours of labor. There are more encouraging signs: Jonas has a lead on a job, and Marija obtains a job painting labels on cans for nearly two dollars a day. Jurgis refuses to allow Teta Elzbieta, Ona, or the children to work. He wants the children to go to school, especially thirteen-year-old Stanislovas. Dede Antanas has no luck finding a job because of his advanced age, and he begins to worry that he is a burden.

The family finds a paper advertising the sale of four-room homes for fifteen hundred dollars. Buyers need only pay three hundred dollars down and the monthly payment is twelve dollars. Ona, Marija, and Teta Elzbieta visit the real estate agent, a slick, well-dressed man who speaks Lithuanian. He tells them that the houses are going fast and that they must move quickly. Later, Ona quickly figures their budget, and it seems that they can make the payments. The entire family makes a trip to see the house. To their disappointment, it doesn't look as new or big as the one in the advertisement. The basement and the attic aren't completely finished. None of the other houses appear occupied. Jokubas later tells them the entire deal is probably a swindle.

Ona and Teta Elzbieta, accompanied by Jokubas, meet the agent to close the deal. Jokubas reads the contract and notices that it refers to the house as a "rental." They get a lawyer but are dismayed to find that he is the agent's friend. He tells them that everything is in order. Ona and Teta Elzbieta close the deal. Jurgis falls into a frenzy when he returns from work and hears the details. He grabs the deed and storms out to find a lawyer, who explains that the house is merely a rental until the purchase price is paid; the house is called a rental to make it easier to evict people who fail to make the monthly payments. Pacified, Jurgis returns home.

Summary: Chapter 5

The family purchases household necessities and settles happily into their home. The pace of work in the slaughterhouse is demanding, but Jurgis doesn't mind; he even enjoys it. He is surprised to find that everyone else hates their jobs and their bosses. Jurgis thinks that they are merely lazy and refuses to join the union, which is lobbying for a reduction in the pace of work.

One man promises Dede Antanas a job in exchange for one-third of his wages. Jurgis speaks to a friend and coworker, Tamoszius Kuszleika, about this practice. Tamoszius explains that corruption exists everywhere in Packingtown. From the top to bottom in the chain of power, people take advantage of one another. It is impossible to move ahead without taking part in the web of graft and corruption. Despite having to sacrifice a third of his wages, Antanas takes the job. He informs the family that he helps pack filthy meat for human consumption.

Marija learns that her job came at the expense of a fifteen-year employee. She also learns that Jonas obtained his job after his predecessor died as a result of the unsafe working conditions. Jurgis notes that unfit meat, such as calf fetuses and animals that have died of disease, are butchered and packed with the rest of the meat.

ANALYSIS: CHAPTERS 3–5

This section continues Sinclair's demolition of the American Dream as he builds his argument against capitalism and for socialism. Jurgis, who still naïvely holds onto the American Dream, views the factories with undiluted optimism. Sinclair portrays him as utterly committed to the values of labor and family on which the American Dream is based. Again, he attempts to make Jurgis appear sympathetic to the average American reader. Unlike Jurgis, the more experienced Jokubas views the entire process with sarcasm because he knows better. He knows the corrupt owners of the vast meatpacking empire betray the values of the American Dream in every way possible.

The vast stockyards, packed with cattle, pigs, and sheep, demonstrate the marvelous efficiency of the economic machinery of the meatpacking industry. However, the animals packed into the stockyards and herded into slaughter serve also as metaphors for the immigrant laborers who crowd into Packingtown looking for the opportunity to earn a piece of the American Dream. Like these ill-fated animals, the unsuspecting Jurgis and other immigrants are herded into the machinery of capitalism and slaughtered en masse.

Sinclair's description of the unsanitary and disgusting practices of the meat-packing industry consists of a two-pronged attack. First, he details the lack of sanitation in the factories in order to garner sympathy for the wage laborers who must work there. But the real impact of his exposé lies in his portrayal of the practice of selling diseased and rotten meat to the American public. Sinclair wants the reader to identify with the immigrant laborer through their victimization by the same enemy. The factory owners value their profits over the health of the workers and the public consumer.

The real-estate scam is another attack on capitalism. The agent lies when he says that the houses are "going fast" to pressure the family into acting without considering all of the conditions. The flyer advertising the houses is misleading. Moreover, the deed specifies that the house is a "rental" until it is paid for. The purpose is to make it easy to evict families when they start missing payments. With its emphasis on maximum profit, the scheme prioritizes corporate gain at the expense of the consumer. A poor family is given no leeway for missed or late payments. Instead, the family is thrown out of its home in times of financial crisis.

Tamoszius's explanation of "graft" to Jurgis portrays capitalism as a machine that encourages and values corruption—anyone hoping to get ahead must become corrupt. Therefore, capitalism attacks the fundamental moral idea behind the American Dream, namely that hard, honest work earns its just reward. Sinclair attempts to show that, within capitalist economics, one cannot advance by means of hard work and a strong commitment to good social values. Instead, the enterprising individual must become a liar, thief, and predator to keep from being exploited.

CHAPTERS 6–9

SUMMARY: CHAPTER 6
Grandmother Majauszkiene, a wizened old Lithuanian neighbor, explains to the family that houses such as the one they have taken are a swindle. She and her son were lucky enough to make the payments long enough to own the house but most people are never able to do so. She explains that the houses are more than fifteen years old and that they were built with the cheapest, shoddiest materials. No one is able to buy the houses because, for the Packingtown workers, missing even one month's payment means eviction and the forfeiture of everything paid on it. The family is shocked to learn that they have to pay interest on their debt, bringing the actual monthly payment close to twenty dollars.

Grandmother Majauszkiene came to Packingtown when the work force was mostly German. The Irish took the Germans' place, and now the Slovaks have taken the place of the Irish. The companies grind down and wear out successive generations of immigrant workers. Four families tried to buy the home that Ona, Jurgis, and their family now live in. One by one, each failed due to the death of a key wage earner through accident or illness.

By paying ten dollars to the forelady, Ona obtains a job sewing covers on hams in a cellar. The young Stanislovas lies about his age and obtains a job working a lard-canning machine.

SUMMARY: CHAPTER 7

Ona and Jurgis's *veselija* has put them over a hundred dollars in debt. Illness strikes the family frequently due to the unsanitary conditions of Packingtown, but no one can take a day off work to recover.

Winter brings bitter cold and impassable snow drifts. The companies don't provide adequate heating at work. There is a wave of death in Packingtown as the bad weather and disease claims the weakened, the hungry, and the old, including Dede Antanas. Thousands wait to take the vacant places in the plants. Many men succumb to the allure of whiskey and beer and become alcoholics. Jurgis resists these temptations because he is determined to shield Ona and their family from the tortures of homelessness and starvation.

SUMMARY: CHAPTER 8

Tamoszius, a musician, begins to court Marija. His fiddle-playing brings a note of cheer into the family's life. He is also a popular guest at various celebrations because he is a musician. He invites Marija to most of them; if the hosts are his friends, he invites the entire family. These celebrations aid the family in surviving the relentless monotony of toil and poverty. Tamoszius proposes to Marija and she accepts. They plan to finish the attic in the house and use it for their room.

Marija's canning factory shuts down and she loses her job. During the winter, after the rush season, many factories close down and many workers lose their jobs. Even Jurgis suffers from a cut-back on the hours at his job. Workers receive no pay for partial hours. The wage earners in the family all join unions. Jurgis begins to recruit other Lithuanians for the union with a zealous fervor, often frustrated by their ignorance and indifference. Their optimism and naïve commitment to the American Dream remind him of the misguided views he held when he first arrived in America.

SUMMARY: CHAPTER 9

Jurgis attends union meetings religiously and resolves to learn English by attending night school and having the children help him.

Jurgis becomes a U.S. citizen at the urging of a man at his plant. He does everything that the man says and follows him to the voting booths and marks the ballot how the man tells him to. For his trouble, Jurgis receives two dollars. Only later does he learn what the entire process means when his fellow union members explain to him that he has been exploited in one of the many vote-buying schemes in the country.

Jurgis learns the folklore of Packingtown. He learns of the graft, corruption, and greed spread by the likes of Mike Scully, a local Irish politician. He hears of the physical injuries and disease that ravage the labor force. He comes to realize that the dishonest meat companies sell diseased meat and label cans as "deviled ham" or "potted ham" although the contents are a mixture of leftover bits and entrails from any number of slaughtered animals.

ANALYSIS: CHAPTERS 6–9

The family's encounter with Grandmother Majauszkiene foreshadows these immigrants' eventual fate. The real-estate companies have trapped them in a scheme by selling them a house that is shiny and pretty on the outside but rotten on the inside. In this way, the house is similar to the tins containing rotten and diseased meats—like these meat products, the house is sold on its appearance. This ruse also exemplifies the betrayal of the American Dream by capitalism. The home is the symbolic center of the family, and owning one's own home is a central tenet of the American Dream. The real-estate company's swindling of Jurgis and his family suggests that the capitalism that makes the American Dream possible also, paradoxically, destroys it.

Grandmother Majauszkiene has seen successive generations of immigrant laborers crowd into Packingtown where they are ground down and worn out. Those who survive enter the web of graft and corruption and, by doing so, advance in power and status, mostly by abusing the next generation of immigrants. The successive waves of wage laborers who come to Packingtown to face abuse and degradation recall the image of the animals being herded to slaughter in the stockyards. These immigrants either fail to succeed or they compromise their moral principles. Either way, as with the ill-fated animals, forces beyond their control determine their respective fates.

An important premise of the novel is that the political and governmental systems that support American capitalism are as rotten and corrupt as the business world itself. Sinclair makes clear that the few labor reform laws aimed at preventing abusive labor practices are largely ineffective. The child labor laws forbidding children under the age of sixteen to work do nothing to keep children from being forced to labor at grueling jobs, since the desperate need for money necessitates that these youths work any job that they can. The very structure of capitalist economics, in Sinclair's portrayal, demands such a sacrifice in order for one to survive. Throughout *The Jungle,* Sinclair uses narrative incidents such as Stanislovas's exploitation as evidence to support the argument that working from within capitalism is not effective. Socialism, he argues, is the only viable political and economic system.

Jurgis's naturalization to become an American citizen, which might otherwise be seen as an encouraging step on his way toward achieving the American Dream, is tainted with corruption. The democratic process is entirely besmirched by politicians with hands caught in the deep pockets of big capitalists. Elections are rigged through an extensive vote-buying scheme, and members of the Chicago criminal underworld take advantage of ignorant, impoverished wage laborers to pervert the democratic process according to the wishes of big businessmen and their cronies.

CHAPTERS 10–13

SUMMARY: CHAPTER 10

> [A] population . . . dependent for its opportunities . . .
> upon the whim of men every bit as brutal and unscru-
> pulous as the old-time slave drivers.
>
> (See QUOTATIONS, p. 53)

Jurgis demands that the agent who sold his family the house reveal all of its hidden expenses. The agent explains that they must pay seven dollars a year for insurance, ten dollars a year in taxes, and six dollars a year for water. He adds that if the city chooses to install a sewer and a sidewalk, they would have to pay between thirty-seven and forty-seven dollars.

Spring arrives and with it come frequent cold rains and mud. In the summer, the factories are infernos. Moreover, legions of flies descend on Packingtown, attracted by the blood and meat. Marija regains her job at the can painting factory, only to lose it two months later. She is fired when she vocally protests being cheated out of a portion of her wages. The loss of her income is devastating to the family because Ona is now expecting Jurgis's child. It takes Marija a month to find work as a beef trimmer. The boss hires her because she is as strong as a man while her wages are half of a man's.

Ona's supervisor, Miss Henderson, the superintendent's jilted mistress, runs a brothel. Her prostitutes get jobs easily in Ona's department. She hates Ona because she is a decent married woman and her toadies make Ona miserable.

Ona gives birth to a healthy boy. She and Jurgis name him Antanas after Jurgis's father. Jurgis is seized with an overpowering affection for his child and his commitment to his role as a family man grows in consequence. But his long work hours prevent him from seeing his son very much. Ona returns to work a week after giving birth, and her health suffers badly.

SUMMARY: CHAPTER 11

The Packingtown laborers are worked at an ever greater speed only to see their wages cut numerous times. Marija opens a bank account for her savings. One morning she discovers that there is a run on the bank. She waits for two days in the line before she can withdraw her money. In truth, her fear is unfounded: an attempt by a policeman to arrest a drunk at the saloon next to the bank drew a crowd, and people who saw the crowd believed that there was a run on the bank, so they hurried to withdraw their money. Marija sews her savings into her clothing, which now weighs her down so that she fears sinking into the mud in the street.

SUMMARY: CHAPTER 12

Jurgis sprains his ankle and cannot return to work for almost three months. The frustration eats away at him and he often vents his bitterness upon his family. His infant son is often the only way for him to return to good humor. Stanislovas suffers frostbite in his hands, and the first joints on his fingers are permanently damaged. Jurgis often has to beat Stanislovas in order to make him go to work on snowy mornings.

Jonas disappears, so the family sends Nikalojus and Vilimas, Teta Elzbieta's ten- and eleven-year-old sons, respectively, to work as newspaper sellers. After a few mishaps, the boys learn the tricks of the trade.

SUMMARY: CHAPTER 13

Teta Elzbieta's youngest child, Kristoforas, dies after eating bad meat. While the old woman is stricken with grief, the rest of the family is relieved, as Kristoforas was congenitally crippled and fussed continually, wearing the nerves of everyone but Teta Elzbieta. Marija loans Teta Elzbieta the money to pay for a real funeral because Jurgis refuses to help.

In the spring, Jurgis looks unsuccessfully for work. He is worn out and unable to attract the boss's eye. He settles for the least desirable job around, a position in a fertilizer mill. The chemicals seep into his skin, making him smell as foul as the muck itself.

The summer brings greater prosperity to the family. Vilimas and Nikalojus, however, begin to acquire bad habits on the streets, so the family sends them back to school. Teta Elzbieta takes a job in a sausage factory. Her thirteen-year-old daughter, Kotrina, takes care of Antanas and her other crippled brother, Juozapas. The bad working conditions wear on Teta Elzbieta's health—she must stand and perform the same repetitive motion for hours on end.

ANALYSIS: CHAPTERS 10–13

In Packingtown, not even the arrival of spring brings cheer to the worker's life. Every season brings with it cause for suffering, which is as relentless as time itself in the wage laborer's world. These chapters illustrate the precarious existence of wage laborers—they are always on the verge of a financial crisis. The injury that incapacitates Jurgis is enough to upset the entire household's stability, forcing others to assume the burden of earning income. The world that Sinclair portrays is remarkably Darwinian, as Jurgis and his family are running a losing race for survival. The conditions of life for them are so harsh that mere survival is considered a success. The weak, the crippled, and the old are weeded out with brutal efficiency.

Capitalists such as those who ran the Chicago stockyards in the early twentieth century often justified brutal labor practices with a philosophy known as Social Darwinism. This philosophy adapts Darwin's theory of evolution to economic struggle, implying that, as in nature, only the fittest and the strongest are meant to survive. According to Social Darwinism, wealthy capitalists were considered the fittest of the human race because they were so successful. The wage laboring class was considered an inferior form of humanity. The widespread racism and prejudice against immigrants helped this belief gain power and influence in turn-of-the-century

American culture. By attributing Jurgis with a strong physique and an initially enthusiastic attitude, Sinclair tries to demonstrate the fiction of Social Darwinism. Capitalism ruins strong, healthy individuals as well as the crippled, the weak, and the old. Only those who are morally corrupt, it seems, survive.

Marija's fear about being weighed down into the mud by her money is a metaphor for the evils of capitalism. Sinclair argues that this system of greed oppresses individuals; here, Marija's coins are a concretized form of money that physically oppresses her. The unassailable primacy of money has conditioned her to guard her money with her life. Marija's quasi-religious devotion to her coins seems to recall Jesus' admonition, according to the New Testament that "[i]t is easier for a camel to go through the eye of a needle, than for a rich man to enter into the kingdom of God" (Matthew 19:24). Though she clutches the money not because she is greedy but because she needs it to survive, Marija has been distorted by capitalism into an un-Christian figure, descending into the mud of base desire.

Throughout these chapters, Sinclair accuses capitalism of undermining the family. Ona has to return to work a mere week after giving birth. She doesn't have the opportunity to be a mother to her child. Almost everyone is happy when the crippled Kristoforas dies because, from a reasoning, mathematical point of view—which is indeed the lens through which these immigrants must examine their lives—the child is a drain on the family's resources, a consumer without being a producer. Jurgis's long work hours prevent the development of a strong bond with his son. The desperate need for sustenance takes priority over sympathy and love, as evidenced by Jurgis's beating of the frostbitten Stanislovas. Jurgis and his family's poverty, a result of capitalist economics, prevent them from being together as a family. Jonas even disappears without warning; it is possible that he dies while at work, but it is more likely that he simply abandons the family, which has deteriorated into a collection of individuals struggling to eke out an existence. Within the capitalist system, families are a burden best avoided if a single individual wishes to survive.

CHAPTERS 14–17

SUMMARY: CHAPTER 14

*[T]here were things that went into the sausage in
comparison with which a poisoned rat was a tidbit.*
(See QUOTATIONS, p. 54)

Jurgis and his family know all of the dirty secrets of the meat-
packing industry. The most spoiled of meats becomes sausage. All
manner of dishonesty exists in the industry's willingness to sell diseased, rotten, and adulterated meat to American households. The
working members of the family fall into a silent stupor due to the
grinding poverty and misery of their lives. Ona and Jurgis grow
apart, and Jurgis begins to drink heavily. He delivers himself from
full-blown alcoholism through force of will, but the desire to drink
always torments him.

Antanas suffers various childhood illnesses, and the measles attack him with fury. His strong constitution allows him to reach his
first birthday, but he is as malnourished as the rest of the Packingtown poor. Ona, pregnant again, develops a bad cough and suffers
increasingly frequent bouts of hysterical crying.

SUMMARY: CHAPTER 15

Winter arrives again, and with it comes the grueling rush season.
Fifteen- and sixteen-hour workdays are frequent. Twice, Ona does
not return home at night. She explains that the snow drifts kept her
away so she stayed with a friend. When Jurgis discovers that she
is lying, he wrangles a confession out of her. Sobbing hysterically,
Ona confesses that Phil Connor, a boss at her factory, continually
harassed her and pleaded with her to become his mistress. She tells
Jurgis that Connor eventually raped her in the factory after everyone had gone home and threatened to arrange the firings of every
wage earner in her household. Moreover, he threatened to prevent
them from obtaining work in Packingtown ever again. With these
threats, he forced her into accompanying him to Miss Henderson's
brothel in the evenings for the past two months.

Jurgis, livid, storms to Ona's workplace. Upon seeing the coarse-
looking and liquor-reeking Connor, he leaps at him and sinks his
fingers into Connor's throat. He channels all of his outrage about
the rape into such a thrashing frenzy that he doesn't even notice the
pandemonium in the factory. A half-dozen men finally tear Jurgis,

blood and skin dripping from his teeth, from the unconscious Connor and take him to the police station.

SUMMARY: CHAPTER 16

> [C]ould they find no better way to punish him than to leave three weak women and six helpless children to starve and freeze?
>
> *(See* QUOTATIONS, *p. 55)*

Jurgis is arrested and taken to jail, where old men and boys, hardened criminals and petty criminals, innocent men and guilty men share the same squalid quarters. A date is designated for Jurgis's trial and his bond is set at three hundred dollars. Afterward, he is taken to the county jail and made to strip; he is then walked, naked, down a hallway past the inmates, who leer and make comments. He is put into a small cell with a filthy, bug-infested mattress. Upon hearing a clanging of bells that evening, Jurgis realizes that it is Christmas Eve. He recalls the previous Christmas, when he and Ona walked along the avenue with the children and gazed at the marvelous food and toys in the store windows. He begins to sob when he thinks of his family spending Christmas without him and with Ona ill. He laments his family's plight and feels that the Christmas chimes are mocking him.

SUMMARY: CHAPTER 17

While Jurgis awaits his trial, he becomes friends with his cellmate, Jack Duane. Jack claims to be an educated man from the east. He says that his father committed suicide after failing in business. He adds that a big company later cheated him out of a lucrative invention. His misfortunes led Jack to become a safe breaker. Before Jurgis's trial, Jack gives Jurgis his mistress's address and encourages him to seek his help should the need arise.

Jurgis's trial is a farce. Kotrina and Teta Elzbieta attend it. Phil Connor testifies that he fired Ona fairly and that Jurgis attacked him for revenge. Jurgis tells his side of the story through an interpreter, but the judge is not sympathetic. He sentences Jurgis to thirty days in prison. Jurgis begs for clemency on the ground that his family will starve if he cannot work, but the judge remains firm.

In Bridewell Prison, Jurgis and the other prisoners spend the greater portion of their time breaking stone. He writes a postcard to his family to let them know where he is. Ten days later, Stanislovas visits to tell him that he, Ona, Marija, and Teta Elzbieta have all lost their jobs and that they are unable to pay rent or buy food. Marija is suffering blood poisoning because she cut her hand at work. Ona lies in bed, crying all day. Teta Elzbieta's sausage factory shut down. Stanislovas lost his job after a snowstorm prevented him from going to work for three days. They cannot obtain other jobs because they are too sick and weak and because Connor is scheming to prevent them from finding work. Stanislovas asks if Jurgis can help them. Jurgis has no more than fourteen cents to give. Kotrina, Stanislovas, and the children earn money selling papers. Their only other income comes from begging.

ANALYSIS: CHAPTERS 14–17

Packingtown is full of predators and, as they have done throughout *The Jungle,* these hostile forces continue to attack the family bond that unites the immigrants. Phil Connor, empowered by his criminal connections, violates the sacred marriage bond between Jurgis and Ona, one of the few things of meaning that the two still possess. The idea of powerlessness pervades this grim section; no poor person has the power to fight for him- or herself. Marija tries to fight for her full wages, only to be fired; Ona cannot afford to reject Connor's advances because he has the power to ruin her family. The wage laborer is systematically crippled and silenced by the power structure of capitalism.

In his attack on Connor, in Chapter 15, Jurgis exhibits an animalistic fury. Sinclair compares him to a "wounded bull" and a "tiger," and the image of Jurgis hovering over Connor with his mouth full of Connor's blood and skin evokes the primal, bestial quality of his rage. Ironically, the factories seek this sort of unrefined animal energy in their workers, which they can channel into efficient labor. Everywhere in Packingtown, there are wage laborers who suffer from some form of permanent disfigurement directly or indirectly related to their work. In a sense, the prevalence of these disfiguring injuries is a metaphor for the butchery of human bodies—which, like animals, are slaughtered in the service of profit.

With Jurgis's sentencing, Sinclair argues that capitalism has perverted the American justice system. Judges are bought and sold by men with power and money, giving impunity to men like Connor. Furthermore, in Jurgis's case, the judge does not care that his ruling means the difference between starvation and survival for an entire family.

Sinclair also charges capitalism with being anti-Christian. Immigrants (both Christian and Jewish) from eastern-European countries held fast to their religious beliefs and traditions upon coming to America as a source of strength and a sense of heritage. Here, however, Jurgis is forced to spend the Christmas holidays separated from his family, and his inability to work leads to them being evicted from their home at a time of year that is traditionally festive. Jurgis's recollection of practically drooling over food and toys in store windows on the previous Christmas pits the harsh and cruel reality of capitalism at odds with the immigrants' fantasies. Jurgis cannot afford the store window contents; his inability to be a consumer marks his failure as a producer, according to the capitalist system.

The family's slew of misfortunes following Jurgis's imprisonment clearly marks the beginning of the family's inevitable descent into ruin. Sinclair foreshadows this fall throughout the early sections of the novel; his commitment to exemplifying the evils of capitalism necessitates that these exploited immigrants fail in their naïve pursuit of the American Dream. Throughout the novel, Sinclair relentlessly insists that hard work, family values, self-reliance, and self-motivated action—the underpinnings of the American Dream—do absolutely nothing to provide the means for social advancement. The wage laborers that populate *The Jungle* are moved inevitably toward ruin and abuse by forces beyond their control. Capitalism becomes a force as inevitable and careless as nature. It picks off unfortunate individuals as carelessly as cold weather, disease, and heat exhaustion.

CHAPTERS 18–21

SUMMARY: CHAPTER 18

Jurgis has to stay in prison for three extra days because he lacks the money to pay the cost of his trial. When he is released, he walks twenty miles to his home in Packingtown. He discovers a new family living in his home. He visits Grandmother Majauszkiene, who informs him that his family could not pay the rent. The agent evicted them and sold the house within a week. She gives him the address of the boarding house where they stayed when they first arrived in Chicago.

Jurgis trudges off toward the old boarding house, feeling defeated and reflecting on how he and his family have been unjustly treated. As the widow stands in the open door, Jurgis hears Ona screaming, and he tears through the house. He hears her in a garret; as he is about to ascend the ladder to the garret, however, Marija tries to stop him. She tells him that the Ona's baby is coming—Ona has gone into premature labor. Unable to stand Ona's horrible cries, Jurgis scrounges together a dollar and a quarter from the widow and other women in her kitchen in order to get help for Ona.

SUMMARY: CHAPTER 19

Jurgis runs to the apartment of a Dutch midwife, Madame Haupt, and begs her to attend to Ona. She asks for twenty-five dollars; after trying unsuccessfully to make her understand that he has neither money nor friends with money, Jurgis heads down the stairs. Madame Haupt finally agrees to go for the dollar and a quarter that Jurgis does have. Marija and the widow turn Jurgis out for the night, telling him that he will only be in the way. He goes to a saloon that he used to frequent, and the saloonkeeper provides him food, drink, and a place to rest. At four o'clock in the morning, Jurgis returns to the boardinghouse and sees Madame Haupt descend from the garret covered in blood. She informs him that the baby is dead and that Ona is dying. Jurgis rushes up to find a priest praying near the withered Ona. She recognizes him for an instant and then dies. In the morning, Kotrina appears and Jurgis demands to know where she has been. She replies that she has been out selling papers with the boys. Jurgis takes three dollars from her and proceeds to a nearby bar to get drunk.

SUMMARY: CHAPTER 20

When Jurgis is sober, Teta Elzbieta begs him to remember Antanas. Jurgis rouses himself to look for work for his son's sake if nothing else. But he soon learns that he is blacklisted in Packingtown. Phil Connor has made certain that he will never find another job there. Marija's hand will soon be healed enough for her to return to work, however, and Teta Elzbieta has a lead on a job scrubbing floors.

After two weeks of futile searching and odd jobs, Jurgis meets an old acquaintance from his union. The man leads him to a factory where harvesting machines are produced, and the foreman gives Jurgis a job. The working conditions are much better, and the factory is a paragon of philanthropy and goodwill. Nevertheless, workers still must keep up a breakneck speed. Jurgis regains hope and begins to make plans, even studying English at night. Several days later, however, a placard at the factory informs the men who work there that Jurgis's department will be closed until further notice.

Summary: Chapter 21

Only the children's wages keep the family from starvation while Jurgis spends more than ten days looking for another job. Juozapas, Teta Elzbieta's crippled child, begins to go to the local dump to find food. A rich woman finds him there and asks him about his life. Hearing of the tragedy and penury that pursues the family, she visits them at the boardinghouse. Shocked at the squalor in which they live, she resolves to find Jurgis a job. She is engaged to be married to a superintendent at a steel mill, so she writes a letter of recommendation for Jurgis. Jurgis takes the letter to the superintendent and gets himself hired.

The mill is too far for Jurgis to return to the boardinghouse during the week, so he travels home only on the weekends. He loves his son with an overwhelming devotion. Antanas's first attempts at speech provide no end of delight to Jurgis. Jurgis begins to read the Sunday paper with the help of the children and settles in a livable routine. But he returns to the boardinghouse one day only to discover that a freak accident has occurred: Antanas has drowned in the mire of mud in the streets.

Analysis: Chapters 18–21

The narrative shape of *The Jungle* is extremely simple: it exposes the fallacy of the American Dream by portraying the gradual destruction of the immigrant family at the hands of the forces of capitalism. Every section, every chapter, and nearly every individual event throughout most of the book operates according to this plan. In this section, not surprisingly, the family continues to suffer greater and greater misfortunes. Their home, the symbol of family life, has been taken from them; the building looks as if the family never even lived there. Jurgis's return to his home is a metaphor for the cyclical nature of generations of immigrants. These waves of immigrants pass through Packingtown and its misery—the only constant in their lives.

Moreover, the second- and third-generation children of earlier waves of immigrants seem to forget that their ancestors suffered the very same abuses that they now perpetrate on the newer generations of immigrants. As theories about eugenics (a science concerned with improving a specific race's hereditary qualities) arose in the late nineteenth century, making claims about the inherent inferiority of nonwhite peoples and white peoples of certain descent, Americans became hostile toward the waves of immigrants whom they perceived as infiltrators spoiling the purity of the American people. The first waves were constituted largely of northern and western Europeans. The Irish, then, stereotyped as potato-eating drunks, were among the early targets of ridicule. With the arrival of later waves of immigrants, largely from southern and eastern Europe, these earlier immigrants sought to take advantage of these new immigrants. Phil Connor, for example, an Irishman, takes part in the abuse and degradation that, a few decades earlier, the Irish suffered at the hands of more powerful ethnic groups. Historical memory is short if not nonexistent in *The Jungle*.

These chapters also function as the next stage of Sinclair's attack on capitalism. Earlier, he shows that child labor laws do nothing to stop child labor, implying that it is not possible to improve working conditions and labor practices from within the structures of capitalism. Jurgis's job at the harvester factory expounds upon the same idea. The factory supposedly functions according to philanthropic values, and the facilities are cleaner and the working conditions more pleasant. Nevertheless, the factory shuts down periodically after the rush season just like other factories, leaving thousands of laborers without the income necessary to survive. The factory's philanthropic values do nothing to change the essentially precarious existence of wage laborers. Again, working from within capitalism fails to provide wage laborers with a secure, decent living.

The young woman who secures Jurgis a job with her recommendation shows compassion in an otherwise cruel world. However, her actions do nothing to change the dangerous working conditions in the steel factory where her fiancé is a superintendent—Jurgis witnesses several men suffer horrendous, disabling accidents in the steel mill. Neither does her kind action make a difference in the dangerous conditions in the slums where wage laborers live. She helps Jurgis secure an income, but Antanas still drowns in the unpaved, muddy streets outside the boarding house. Through this example, Sinclair argues, pessimistically, that individual philanthropists working within the structures of capitalism are likewise ineffective at changing the lives of wage laborers for the better.

CHAPTERS 22–24

SUMMARY: CHAPTER 22

Jurgis looks at Antanas's dead body and leaves the house without a word. He walks to the nearest railway crossing and hides in a car.

During his journey, he fights every sign of grief and emotion. He regards his experiences up until now as a lengthy nightmare that he has had to endure. He rides the railway car into the country. The clean air and space revive him, and he jumps off when the train stops. He bathes and washes his clothes in the nearest stream. He tries to buy food at a farmhouse but the farmer sends him away because he doesn't feed "tramps." Jurgis makes his way across the farmer's field, ripping up a hundred young peach trees in response.

Another farmer is kind enough to sell Jurgis a dinner and let him sleep in the barn. He offers Jurgis work; Jurgis asks if there is enough to last all winter. The farmer says that he can guarantee work only through November. Jurgis sarcastically asks if he turns his horses out for the winter as well since they are useful for only part of the year. The farmer asks why a strong man cannot find work in the cities in the winter. Jurgis explains that everyone thinks that there must be work in the city in the winter and that the cities therefore become overcrowded. As a result, many of these laborers end up having to steal and beg in order to survive. Jurgis turns down the farmer's offer of work and continues on his way.

Jurgis earns a few meals with odd jobs, stealing and foraging when he isn't working. After a while, he stops asking for shelter from farmers because so many are hostile to him. He feels like his own master again. He learns a few tricks and secrets from the other tramps in the countryside. Farmers are almost frantic for help during this season, and work is easy to find. Jurgis works for two weeks and receives a sum that he would have earlier considered a fortune. He spends all of it on alcohol and women in one night, and his own conscience judges him mercilessly for this waste.

SUMMARY: CHAPTER 23

Jurgis returns to Chicago in the fall because the cold weather is upon him. He finds a job digging underground tunnels for railway freight. The purpose of the tunnels is to break the power of the teamster's union, though Jurgis remains unaware of this goal for a year. Confident that the job will last all winter, he spends his money on alcohol with abandon. Unfortunately, however, he suffers an accident and breaks his arm. He spends Christmas in the hospital. After two weeks, he is ushered out of the hospital, to his dismay. It is the dead of winter. He attends a religious revival with other bums just to stay warm. He despises the men preaching at the revival since he feels that they have no right to talk about saving souls when men like him only need a "decent existence for their bodies."

SUMMARY: CHAPTER 24

That winter, work is scarcer than ever before, and Jurgis must fiercely compete with the other homeless poor for the hiding places and warmth in saloons. One night, while begging, he happens upon a very drunk, well-dressed young man named Freddie Jones. Jones invites him to his house for a meal and offers to pay for the cab ride there. He hands a bill to Jurgis and tells him to pay the cabbie and keep the change for himself. Jurgis finds that it is a one-hundred-dollar bill. The opulence and luxury of Freddie's mansion astound Jurgis. He learns from Freddie's drunken rambling that he is the son of "Jones the packer." Jurgis realizes that the elder Jones owns the factory where he first worked in Packingtown. Freddie gives Jurgis a large dinner despite the obvious disapproval of the butler, Hamilton. Once Freddie falls to sleep, Hamilton orders Jurgis to leave. Hamilton tries to search him, but Jurgis threatens to fight if Hamilton lays a finger on him.

ANALYSIS: CHAPTERS 22–24

As Sinclair portrays the destruction of the immigrant family through the brutal machinery of turn-of-the-century capitalism, he continues to focus principally on the development of Jurgis's character. The accumulated tragedies in his life have emptied his emotional reserves, as evidenced by his inability to grieve adequately for his son. This final blow compels him to abandon the moral and social principles (such as loyalty to family) to which he has thus far clung and instead adopt the dog-eat-dog values of the world in which he lives. According to this new outlook, if someone deals him a blow, he deals one back. When the farmer refuses to sell him a meal, Jurgis responds by vandalizing his property, tearing up his newly planted peach trees. The conditions of poverty and misery created by capitalism have annihilated his ability to invest emotionally in his family, and he abandons Teta Elzbieta, Marija, and the other children because he does not have the emotional reserves to watch them sink, either literally or figuratively, into ruin. Without this crucial anchor, Jurgis gives himself over to complete debauchery—Sinclair again positions capitalism as a threat to fundamental American values.

The religious revival serves as an attack on the misdirected efforts of organized religion. Like the misdirected philanthropy of the rich woman in Chapter 21, Christianity here does nothing to improve the lives of wage laborers. It preaches morality but fails to provide the material conditions necessary for one to be a moral person.

Jurgis's encounter with Freddie Jones is obviously meant to illustrate the vast difference in standard of living between employers and the wage laborers who work for them. Jones is a drunken, wasteful fop who hands out one-hundred-dollar bills as if they were nothing; he has no conception of the value of money. Moreover, the luxury and opulence of Freddie's home illustrate his father's extravagant waste of the wealth generated through wage slavery. This disparity between a laborer such as Jurgis, who has long worked in grueling conditions with virtually no reward, and Freddie, who has certainly never had to face anything remotely resembling Jurgis's ghastly reality but who nonetheless reaps the benefit of hard work—*others'* hard work—is a crystal clear manifestation of Sinclair's advocacy of socialism and equal distribution of wealth.

Occasionally, Sinclair's political fervor overwhelms the stylistic constraints that he has set for himself. The realist style that Sinclair uses to expose appalling working conditions requires consistent adherence throughout the text because deviation from it reveals the text to be contrived. The horror of the packing plant loses its rhetorical force if other events are not believable. For example, Sinclair's realism falters in the dialogue between Jurgis and Freddie. Sinclair renders the speech of the drunken Freddie with a consummate, almost exaggerated, realism. He stutters, slurs his speech, and wanders from thought to thought. Jurgis's dialogue, conversely, is idealized. When the butler begins to threaten "I'll have the police—", Jurgis interjects with a clever play on words, shouting "Have 'em!" This pun on the word "have" seems beyond the language skills of an uneducated Lithuanian immigrant. Similarly, Jurgis's cry, "I'll not have you touch me!" seems too polished for someone of his social status. The inconsistent treatment of dialogue in this example mirrors the inconsistent realism in the text as a whole. Sinclair places capitalists and capitalism under a glaring spotlight and reports every ugly detail; however, he spares his protagonist and the working classes realistic treatment that might reflect poorly on them. They are often glorified, idealized, and flattened into one-dimensional types.

CHAPTERS 25–26

SUMMARY: CHAPTER 25

Jurgis quickly realizes that he cannot get change for a one-hundred-dollar bill without raising suspicions or being robbed. He enters a saloon to try anyway. The bartender tells Jurgis that he must buy a drink first. Jurgis agrees to have a glass of beer for five cents. The bartender takes the bill and gives him ninety-five cents in change. Realizing that he has been cheated, Jurgis furiously attacks the bartender. A policeman rushes in and drags Jurgis to jail. The judge at his trial finds Jurgis's version of events laughable. He sentences Jurgis to ten days in jail plus costs.

Jurgis again encounters Jack Duane in Bridewell Prison. Jurgis agrees to see Duane when he gets out of jail. Jurgis listens to the other prisoners and decides that a life of crime is the best way to survive. He visits Jack at a pawnshop where he is hiding out, and Jack takes him on his first mugging. They attack a well-dressed man and steal his jewelry and wallet. Jurgis's share is fifty-five dollars. Jurgis reads in the paper that the victim suffered a concussion and nearly froze to death while he was unconscious; he will lose three fingers to frostbite. Over time, Jurgis ceases to worry about what happens to his victims.

Through Duane, Jurgis becomes acquainted with Chicago's criminal underground. On one outing, a watchman catches Duane breaking a safe. A policeman allows him to escape, but it causes such a scandal that Duane's criminal associates choose to sacrifice him. Duane then flees Chicago. Meanwhile, Jurgis begins talking with Harper, a vote-buyer for the corrupt politicians of Chicago. An election is coming up, and Harper offers to let Jurgis take part in the schemes. Harper introduces him to Mike Scully, a wealthy, corrupt democrat. Scully wants Jurgis to take a job in the stockyards and join a union. Scully and the Republicans have made a pact, and Scully wants Jurgis to support a Republican candidate.

Jurgis takes a job as a hog trimmer for which he receives regular pay in addition to the fruits of political graft. He works tirelessly for the Republican candidate and, when it comes time to vote, ushers group after group of immigrant workers through the polls. The Republican candidate is elected to office and Jurgis becomes three hundred dollars richer. He treats himself to a long drinking binge. Meanwhile, Packingtown is alive with celebration over the political victory.

SUMMARY: CHAPTER 26

> [T]he blazing midsummer sun beat down upon that
> square mile of abominations . . . rivers of hot blood
> and carloads of moist flesh . . .
>
> (See QUOTATIONS, p. 56)

Jurgis keeps his job as a hog trimmer. In May, the unions and the packers clash and a huge strike begins. Scully denounces the packers in the papers, so Jurgis asks for another job while he strikes with the rest. Scully tells him to be a scab and make as much as he can out of it. Jurgis argues for a wage of three dollars a day and receives it. The packers hire all of the thugs in the city and import scabs from all over the country, including a significant number of southern blacks.

Jurgis is offered a position as a boss on the killing beds. The packers are desperate to provide fresh meat in order to keep public opinion from turning against them. Jurgis receives a higher wage and the promise that he will have the job after the strike. Nevertheless, the packers feel pressure from the public to settle. They reach an agreement with the union, but the packers break their promise to not discriminate against union leaders. In response, the workers return to striking. During the storm of debauchery that follows, Jurgis comes face to face with Phil Connor in Packingtown. Without thinking, he viciously attacks Connor. Jurgis calls Harper from his jail cell only to discover that Connor is one of Scully's favorites. Harper can do nothing for him except get his bail lowered so that Jurgis can pay it. He advises Jurgis to skip town. Jurgis pays his bail, which leaves him with less than four dollars, and he travels to the other end of Chicago.

ANALYSIS: CHAPTERS 25–26

Jurgis's entrance into the underworld of crime demonstrates that merciless predation, thievery, and dishonesty are far better rewarded in the universe of *The Jungle* than commitment to fundamental American values. It also provides a look into the corruption of the justice system and the democratic political process. Jurgis makes far more money by mugging, rigging elections, and working as a scab than he did as a regular wage earner. Sinclair again ironically positions capitalism, which is generally considered to be the forum of the American Dream, as a threat to the American way. Whereas Jurgis earlier fails to achieve this dream when he submits himself wholeheartedly to the process that he believes will garner him that life for which he longs, he now succeeds by means of tactics antithetical to the values of hard work and honesty. The profits that he makes from these practices assuages his conscience, so that he cares only about himself and can completely ignore the suffering of his victims, just as the real estate agent and various foremen earlier ignore his suffering.

Jurgis heads down the road of corruption and dishonesty, and Sinclair uses the encounter with Phil Connor to illustrate that any remaining vestige of morality or desire to achieve the American Dream by honest means is pointless for Jurgis. His instinctive attack on Connor evidences a lingering sense of injustice at Connor's rape of Ona. But though this sentiment may be somewhat noble, it only lands him in prison again, which inevitably leads to his losing all of his money again. Sinclair, thus, reasserts the worthlessness of moral values in the face of capitalism, as one cannot gain ground by clinging to such idealistic values when corruption abounds.

In particular, Sinclair focuses on the moral depredations of capitalism, especially the corrupting influence of vice among the laborers as a means of escaping the miseries of their lives. He describes the depravity and immorality that run unchecked among the scab workers in order to charge the meat packers with encouraging sinful behavior. Gambling, fighting, and prostitution run rampant in the population of scab workers. He describes how these prostitutes, criminals, and gamblers handle the meat that is sold to the American public. Sinclair equates the moral "dirtiness" of the scab workers with the literal dirtiness of the meat itself.

Sinclair's representation of the scab workers attacks the meat packers by association. The filth and immorality of the scabs rubs off on their employers. However, the racism prevalent in turn-of-the-century white America begins to creep into Sinclair's narrative at this stage. Many of the scab workers are black southerners, to whom Sinclair often refers as "big buck Negroes." The black scab workers are continually described as lazy, ignorant, criminal, and self-destructive. Furthermore, he conjures images of these "big buck Negroes" rubbing elbows with white country girls, knowing that the idea of black men cavorting with white women would raise the ire of white readers. Sinclair states that their ancestors were once African savages forced into slavery; now, however, they are really "free" for the first time—"free to wreck themselves." In his fervent attempt to rouse the reading public's moral outrage against big capitalists, Sinclair reproduces, unfortunately, some of the most racist stereotypes against blacks.

CHAPTERS 27–28

SUMMARY: CHAPTER 27

Jurgis begins begging for a job. Unfortunately, the strike ends just as he is at his most desperate. The labor imported during the strike adds more men to the crowds searching for work. Moreover, his standard of living increased exponentially when money came easily to him, so the return to homeless begging hits him hard. He eventually obtains a job only to be fired because he is not strong enough for the work. Winter approaches, and election time arrives again. Jurgis watches bitterly as the graft continues while he can no longer take part in it. He attends a political meeting where he can stay warm, but a policeman throws him out after he falls asleep and begins to snore.

While begging for the price of a night's lodging, Jurgis encounters a woman he knew from his first years in Packingtown. She is well-dressed now. She does not have any money with her, but she gives him Marija's address. She urges Jurgis to visit Marija and Teta Elzbieta. She assures him that they will be happy to see him. Jurgis hurries to see Marija. When he enters the building, the police raid the establishment. Jurgis realizes that it is a brothel.

Jurgis spots Marija, and they manage to talk a bit before the police herd them into the police station. Marija explains that neither she nor Teta Elzbieta could support the children with legitimate jobs. She adds that, moreover, Stanislovas died: he fell asleep in the storeroom of an oil factory and a swarm of rats attacked him and killed him. Marija then chose to go into prostitution in order to keep the rest of the family from starvation. She assures Jurgis that they never blamed him for running away and that they know that he did his best. The knowledge of Marija's shame and Stanislovas's horrible death haunts Jurgis throughout the night, which he spends in jail.

SUMMARY: CHAPTER 28

The madam of the brothel pays Marija's fine and the prostitutes are set free. The judge lets Jurgis go without penalty because Jurgis says that he had gone merely to visit his sister. He gives a false name at his arrest, and no one recognizes him as Phil Connor's attacker. Marija later confesses that she is a morphine addict. Most of the prostitutes, she tells Jurgis, are addicted to something. She explains that women are kidnapped and forced into the work and that they cannot leave because the madam keeps them in debt and addicted to drugs. Marija gives Jurgis Teta Elzbieta's address and urges him to stay with her and her remaining children. Jurgis doesn't want to see her until he gets a job because he feels guilty for leaving them after Antanas died.

Jurgis spends the rest of the day looking for work. He eats dinner and, while walking the streets, chances upon a political meeting. He enters the hall to sit and rest while he ponders how Teta Elzbieta will receive him. He fears her condemnation and the possibility that she may think that he merely wants to loaf at her expense. He begins to nod off during the speech. A well-dressed woman calls him "comrade" and urges him to listen to the speech. No one tries to throw him out for sleeping.

Jurgis listens to the speech; he has wandered into a socialist political meeting. The speaker details the miserable conditions of life for the common worker. He points out the corrupt practices of big capitalists to grind common laborers into submission. Jurgis finds the expression of all of his misery in the man's speech. He enters an exultation of joy listening to the rousing words of the speaker. He finds confirmation of everything that he has suffered and everything that he has seen. For the first time, he has found a political party to represent his interests rather than those of the privileged, powerful, and wealthy.

Analysis: Chapters 27–28

Marija's entrance into prostitution culminates the essential accusation that Sinclair levels against capitalism: throughout *The Jungle,* he charges capitalism with trafficking in human lives. Human beings are despicably regarded as useful resources—means to an end rather than individuals—and are used until they are worn out and then ultimately thrown away. As a prostitute, Marija epitomizes this trafficking in human bodies, as society's perception of her worth lies wholly in her ability to satisfy the basest desires of humankind. Just as the prostitutes are kept in a form of slavery, Sinclair often compares wage laborers to slaves, another form of trafficking in human bodies. Throughout the novel, human lives are bought and sold, although most wage laborers don't even realize that they are part of a vast market of human flesh.

To this point, the meaning of the title *The Jungle* has been made painfully clear: the world of the wage laborer is a savage realm characterized by a Darwinian struggle for survival. Those who refuse to sacrifice their humanity, integrity, and individuality do not survive, much less succeed, in this world. New arrivals enter into this jungle crammed with predators waiting to attack them at every turn. The structures of capitalism are a jungle of hidden nooks and crannies, each containing yet another dirty secret. Sinclair's novel exposes the various levels of deception within the factories as well as the day-to-day details of the wage laborer's life. He probes the courtroom, prison, and criminal underworld in order to show the far reach of capitalism's structures of power.

Having gone to such great lengths to illustrate the evils of capitalism, Sinclair now offers socialism as the solution to the problems that the first twenty-seven chapters of the novel have explored in detail. When Jurgis enters the socialist political meeting in Chapter 28, he is a defeated man: he has tried all forms of survival but none has offered the security and the peace of mind that he seeks. The socialist political meeting, however, proves anything but a jungle; rather, it is a haven from the cruel reality of capitalism. The rude awakening at the hands of an unsympathetic policeman is replaced by the gentle nudge of one who wants him to better himself by understanding the socialist message. That this woman addresses him as "comrade" demonstrates her desire for them to be equal, which shocks Jurgis; that she is beautiful and well-dressed pits her against all of the wealthy capitalists who ignore the suffering of the common laborer.

As the speaker catalogues the abuses and suffering of wage laborers, Jurgis reacts to socialism like a new, devout religious convert. Unlike the preacher at the religious revival meeting, who wanted commoners to better themselves according to the existing system, the socialist speaker wants commoners to motivate for change *outside* the system. He understands Jurgis's experiences and addresses Jurgis's needs rather than those of the wealthy. For the first time in America, Jurgis feels that he is no longer alone; just as he earlier gives himself to the quasi-religious pursuit of the American Dream, he is now willing to give himself to this camaraderie.

CHAPTERS 29–31

SUMMARY: CHAPTER 29

> *To Jurgis the packers had been equivalent to fate;*
> *Ostrinski showed him that they were . . . a gigantic*
> *combination of capital.*
>
> *(See* QUOTATIONS, *p. 57)*

After the meeting ends, Jurgis finds the speaker resting amid a crowd of people. He asks for more information about the party, and the speaker directs him to Ostrinski, a socialist who speaks Lithuanian. Ostrinski takes Jurgis to his home. They share their experiences in scraping out a miserable existence. Ostrinski explains that wage-earners have nothing but their labor to sell. None of them can obtain a price for it that is higher than what the most desperate worker will take.

Ostrinski explains that there are two economic classes: the small, privileged capitalist class and the large, impoverished proletariat. Because the capitalists are few in number, they can easily work together in favor of their own interests. The proletariat, on the other hand, is large and generally ignorant. Ostrinski explains that workers need to gain "class consciousness" so that they can organize in favor of their interests. In this way, they can avoid the merciless wage competition. Ostrinski calls the current system "wage slavery." Although America claims to be the land of the free, Ostrinski explains that political freedom doesn't alleviate the grinding misery of wage slavery. He adds that socialism is necessarily a worldwide movement: any one nation that achieves success will be crushed by the others around it. Ostrinski calls socialism the "new religion" of humanity. He adds that it could also be interpreted as the fulfillment of Christian values on Earth.

SUMMARY: CHAPTER 30

Jurgis visits Teta Elzbieta to tell her about socialism. She is happy to hear that he wishes to work and help support the family. She even agrees to attend socialist political meetings with him from time to time. Jurgis finds a job as a porter in a small hotel that pays thirty dollars a month plus board. Ostrinski informs Jurgis that his new boss, Tommy Hinds, is actually a state organizer for the socialist party and a well-known socialist speaker. Hinds is overjoyed to find that Jurgis is a comrade. Hinds never tires of preaching socialism in his hotel and elsewhere. Socialists flock to the hotel, so the radical philosophy of the proprietor does not hurt the business he owns. Hinds often urges Jurgis to detail the horrendous filth of the meat-packing plants along with the real recipes for tinned meats and sausages.

Jurgis takes up the socialist cause with a passion. He endeavors to read newspapers, including *The Appeal to Reason,* and learn all about the political and economic systems of power in America. He becomes angry and frustrated when he cannot sway people to socialism.

SUMMARY: CHAPTER 31

Jurgis attempts to persuade Marija to leave prostitution, but she explains that she cannot because she is addicted to morphine. She plans to remain a prostitute for the rest of her life.

Jurgis attends a meeting with a magazine editor who opposes socialism but has agreed to listen to some proponents of the movement. Jurgis's role is to detail the unsanitary conditions under which meat is packed and sold to the public. Nicholas Schliemann, a fierce socialist, explains that the movement wishes to enact public ownership of the means of production. Once the inefficiency of production is eliminated through science and eradication of graft, no worker will be obliged to labor for countless hours a day merely to survive. He can work as little as two hours a day and devote the rest of his time to his personal interests.

The basic goals of socialism are "common ownership and democratic management of the means of producing the necessities of life." The means to bring about this revolution is to raise the class consciousness of the proletariat around the world through political organization. Later, the socialist party achieves phenomenal victories in the elections across the country. A spirited speaker at a political meeting urges socialists to continue fighting because the victory is not yet won, encouraging them with the words, "Chicago will be ours!"

ANALYSIS: CHAPTERS 29–31

The final chapters of *The Jungle* largely abandon the narrative, functioning as an explanation and an argument for socialism. Insofar as they tell a story, it is the story of Jurgis's process of conversion to socialism. The newly introduced Ostrinski and Schliemann are less dramatic characters than mouthpieces for socialism. The ending of

The Jungle is, to a great extent, meant to be simplistic. Sinclair's aim, after all, is not to present the complicated nuances of actual political and economic practices but to persuade the reader to adopt his opinions. The lack of literary sophistication in the ending is obvious, but it is also questionable whether the simplistic ending and the one-dimensional story in general make for the most persuasive political argument. One can argue that the credibility of the novel as reportage becomes doubtful as it begins to resemble propaganda. Sinclair closes his sharp eye for detail when he examines socialism, and the effect stunts the humanity of the people whom he wants to liberate. Ironically, the peoples' movement seems devoid of real human beings. If Sinclair wants the reader to identify with his socialists, he fails because there is no real human being with whom to identify. Jurgis, a constricted character to begin with, almost disappears, and the new characters are flatter than any that Sinclair has offered so far.

The shift to pure propaganda in the final chapters occasions several awkward ruptures in the narrative perspective. Throughout *The Jungle,* Sinclair narrates events as seen through the eyes of Jurgis, though he sometimes employs a more omniscient perspective to describe business dealings and social problems that Jurgis doesn't witness. In an attempt to weave these passages into the narrative fabric, Sinclair has Jurgis learn of them at some unspecified future point in time. As the volume of political argument increases in the final chapters, the interweaving of political commentary and narrative structure becomes more forced. Sinclair recounts that "after Jurgis had made himself more familiar with the Socialist literature, as he would very quickly, he would get glimpses of the Beef Trust from all sorts of aspects . . ."; a lengthy polemic against the Beef Trust then follows, as if it comprises the knowledge that Sinclair claims that Jurgis gains.

The meetings that Jurgis attends provide another forum for Sinclair to air his politics, as does the literature that Jurgis reads. These framing devices are sites of tension between Sinclair's politics and the demands of literary composition. Sinclair wants to make his argument in as blunt a language as possible, but the work of fiction has its own laws of internal consistency. The journalistic style that Sinclair employs requires realism. Moreover, a narrative perspective that filters events and ideas through the experience of the protagonist must do so consistently or risk breaking apart. The framing devices show that Sinclair feels these demands. He knows that information about the Beef Trust cannot simply be inserted into the text; rather, its presence has to be justified in the narrative structure. Thus, Jurgis learns about the Beef Trust at some future, unspecified point, and Sinclair is free to rail against it.

One can argue again, however, that these framing devices are too cheap to be effective. They are usually a single sentence, an afterthought. Perhaps their real failure, though, lies in the fact that they do not control the information that follows. They claim that what follows is witnessed or learned by Jurgis, but Jurgis's perspective disappears in the subsequent argument. The reader doesn't learn how Jurgis, in particular, receives what he learns from socialist literature. Jurgis doesn't filter events and information through his subjectivity; he is simply a conduit: "Such was the home in which Jurgis lived and worked. . . ." His character, one might argue, becomes not only flat but hollow.

IMPORTANT QUOTATIONS EXPLAINED

1. Here was a population, low-class and mostly foreign, hanging always on the verge of starvation, and dependent for its opportunities of life upon the whim of men every bit as brutal and unscrupulous as the old-time slave drivers; under such circumstances immorality was exactly as inevitable, and as prevalent, as it was under the system of chattel slavery. Things that were quite unspeakable went on there in the packing houses all the time, and were taken for granted by everybody; only they did not show, as in the old slavery times, because there was no difference in color between master and slave.

This quote from Chapter 10 comes from Sinclair's explanation of Ona's working conditions; she is forced to work under Miss Henderson, who runs a prostitution ring, and most of her coworkers are prostitutes. Sinclair presents these conditions as a horrible situation for the modest, moral Ona but also offers an explanation in which the system of prostitution is examined in rough economic terms. As with every other failing among the working class in the novel, prostitution is shown not as an innate fault of the women involved but rather as the fault of the capitalists and the economic oppression that they force upon the impoverished immigrants. This passage also hints at the sexual oppression that young working girls are forced to endure from their bosses and foreshadows Ona's rape at the hands of Phil Connor.

Additionally, the last sentence raises a Marxist argument about the appearance of calm surrounding social relations under capitalism. The argument runs that social relations under capitalism are no less exploitative than those that existed under slavery and in feudal societies but that capitalism conceals the true turbulent nature of these relationships under a veneer of naturalness and inevitability. The difference between wage labor and these antiquated forms of subjugation is only a matter of transparency; though the "difference in color between master and slave" is no longer applicable to the owner-laborer relationship, the oppression remains the same.

2. [T]he meat would be shoveled into carts, and the man who did the shoveling would not trouble to lift out a rat even when he saw one—there were things that went into the sausage in comparison with which a poisoned rat was a tidbit. There was no place for the men to wash their hands before they ate their dinner, and so they made a practice of washing them in the water that was to be ladled into the sausage. There were the butt-ends of smoked meat, and the scraps of corned beef, and all the odds and ends of the waste of the plants, that would be dumped into old barrels in the cellar and left there. Under the system of rigid economy which the packers enforced, there were some jobs that it only paid to do once in a long time, and among these was the cleaning out of the waste barrels. Every spring they did it; and in the barrels would be dirt and rust and old nails and stale water—and cartload after cartload of it would be taken up and dumped into the hoppers with fresh meat, and sent out to the public's breakfast.

This long description from Chapter 14 is among the most famous and influential passages in the novel and helps to explain why the book caused so much public furor upon its publication. Sinclair intended the book to raise public consciousness about the plight of the working poor, but he relied on a pseudo-naturalistic technique that emphasized the physically revolting filth and gore of the stockyards. As a result, the novel caused outrage about the unsanitary quality of the meat that was sold in stores rather than the oppression of the poor. The public pressed less for the socialist reforms that Sinclair backed than the public reform to food laws. The image of all kinds of waste being dumped in with the consumer's product is surely revolting; that it is dumped in without any regard for the consumer by greedy capitalists is infuriating. Sinclair himself stated: "I aimed at the public's heart, and by accident I hit it in the stomach."

3. They put him in a place where the snow could not beat in, where the cold could not eat through his bones; they brought him food and drink—why, in the name of heaven, if they must punish him, did they not put his family in jail and leave him outside—why could they find no better way to punish him than to leave three weak women and six helpless children to starve and freeze?

This quote from Chapter 16 explains Jurgis's mindset when he is sent to prison after attacking Phil Connor. Ironically, to Jurgis, the prison is actually an environment far preferable to the cruel, filthy world of Packingtown. Here he receives shelter from the elements and food without having to do anything; he believes that his family members are the real prisoners, as, without his support, they now face starvation and eviction. It is a measure of Jurgis's sympathy and of the horrible conditions that the family is forced to endure that Jurgis actually wishes that his family were sent to prison in his place. Additionally, Jurgis's rhetorical question at the end of the quote speaks to the cold and unsympathetic nature of capitalism: if the women and children cannot earn the means to survive, it is because they aren't productive enough as laborers.

QUOTATIONS

4. All day long the blazing midsummer sun beat down upon
    that square mile of abominations: upon tens of thousands
    of cattle crowded into pens whose wooden floors stank and
    steamed contagion; upon bare, blistering, cinder-strewn
    railroad tracks, and huge blocks of dingy meat factories,
    whose labyrinthine passages defied a breath of fresh air
    to penetrate them; and there were not merely rivers of hot
    blood, and carloads of moist flesh, and rendering vats and
    soap caldrons, glue factories and fertilizer tanks, that smelt
    like the craters of hell—there were also tons of garbage
    festering in the sun, and the greasy laundry of the workers
    hung out to dry, and dining rooms littered with food and
    black with flies, and toilet rooms that were open sewers.

This descriptive passage from Chapter 26 portrays the rank and
festering physical environment in which the Packingtown laborers
are forced to live, helping to explain why Jurgis found prison so
preferable. The passage also shows off the lurid, pseudo-naturalistic
style that Sinclair adopted for the novel, which matches his flair for
physical description with his desire to shock and disgust his readers. He captures the disgusting filth and general unbearableness of
Packingtown in the images of "floors [that] stank and steamed con-
tagion" and "blistering . . . railroad tracks." Furthermore, he breaks
down the meat-packing plant into the raw, nauseating elements of
"rivers of hot blood" and "carloads of moist flesh." This repulsive-
ness plagues not only the factories but also the laborers and their
living quarters; they have "greasy laundry" and sordid bathrooms.
Sinclair deliberately makes his readers feel uncomfortable in the
hopes of stirring up their sympathy, and *The Jungle* is full of vivid
and stomach-churning passages such as this one.

QUOTATIONS

5.   To Jurgis the packers had been equivalent to fate; Ostrinski
      showed him that they were the Beef Trust. They were a
      gigantic combination of capital, which had crushed all
      opposition, and overthrown the laws of the land, and was
      preying upon the people.

This quote from Chapter 29 illustrates the effect of Jurgis's adoption
of socialism upon his mind. He previously considers the capitalists
"equivalent to fate," believing them to be all-powerful, impersonal,
inhuman forces that have total control over his life. But Ostrinski
convinces him that the capitalists are merely corrupt human beings
who immorally oppress other human beings. Jurgis realizes here
that the only difference between the capitalists and the workers lies
in money, for while the capitalists have "a gigantic combination of
capital," the workers have nothing. But, as the speech at the end of
the novel emphasizes, there are many more workers than capitalists,
which could enable the socialist party to overthrow the hegemony
of capitalism in a democratic system. This quote demonstrates the
opening of Jurgis's mind to politics and economics, as he takes up
the socialist cause with a fervor at least as strong as that with which
he initially embraces capitalism and the American Dream.

QUOTATIONS

KEY FACTS

FULL TITLE
The Jungle

AUTHOR
Upton Sinclair

TYPE OF WORK
Novel

GENRE
Social criticism, political fiction, muckraking fiction

LANGUAGE
English

TIME AND PLACE WRITTEN
1905–1906, Chicago and Princeton, New Jersey

DATE OF FIRST PUBLICATION
1906

PUBLISHER
Sinclair published the novel at his own expense after several
publishing firms rejected it.

NARRATOR
Though the narrator is anonymous, his sympathy for the
laborers and vilification of capitalists identifies him as Sinclair's
mouthpiece.

POINT OF VIEW
The third-person narrator focuses on what Jurgis Rudkus
does and what he feels, learns, and experiences. The quasi-
omniscient narrator also provides commentary on the
social forces that affect characters' lives, though often this
commentary is framed as knowledge that Jurgis gains at some
future point.

TONE
Sinclair's attitude toward the story is obvious: the victimized
working class is righteous, and the oppressing capitalists are
evil. Sinclair's perspective is identical to that of the narrator.

TENSE
Past

SETTING (TIME)
Early 1900s

SETTING (PLACE)
Packingtown, the meat-packing sector of Chicago

PROTAGONIST
Jurgis

MAJOR CONFLICT
Jurgis and his family attempt to pursue the American Dream, but wage slavery and the oppression of capitalism shatter every aspect of their lives.

RISING ACTION
Phil Connor's rape of Ona; Jurgis's having to spend Christmas in jail away from his family; Ona's death during childbirth

CLIMAX
Upon hearing of Antanas's death, in Chapter 21, Jurgis feels destroyed by capitalism.

FALLING ACTION
Jurgis's abandonment of his family and turn to dishonest means to survive; Marija's turn to prostitution

THEMES
Socialism as a remedy for the evils of capitalism; the immigrant experience and the hollowness of the American Dream

MOTIFS
Corruption; family and tradition

SYMBOLS
Packingtown and the stockyards symbolize the exploitation of workers; the idea of the jungle symbolizes the capitalist idea of the survival of the fittest; cans of rotten meat symbolize the disingenuous face of capitalism; Teta Elzbieta symbolizes the family, while Jonas symbolizes capitalism's destruction of the family.

FORESHADOWING

The grim setting of Packingtown foreshadows the family's eventual destruction; the conversation with Grandmother Majauszkiene about the housing swindle foreshadows their eviction; Jurgis's experiences with vote-buying and crime early in the novel foreshadow his later participation in similar schemes.

STUDY QUESTIONS

1. *How does Sinclair depict the failure of attempts to improve wage laborers' lives by working from within capitalism? Think especially about legal, social, and philanthropic efforts.*

Sinclair argues that meaningful change cannot be effected from within the system of capitalism because of the fundamental and endless need for money. In the world of *The Jungle,* child labor laws don't bring an end to child labor—wage laborers must keep their children working because they cannot survive without this additional income. The owners of the harvester factory in which Jurgis works make an attempt to provide more pleasant working conditions than most factories. But the factory shuts down periodically after the rush season just like the other factories, leaving thousands of laborers without the necessary income to survive. The factory's enriching qualities thus do nothing to change the precarious existence of wage laborers: the essential relationship between the capitalist who needs big profit margins and the laborer whom the capitalist hires as a means to that end remains intact. Again, working from within capitalism fails to provide wage laborers with a secure, decent living. Similarly, the recommendation that Jurgis gets from a young woman, though it secures him a job, doesn't remedy the steel mill's dangerous working conditions. Sinclair's chief contention is that the working class cannot rise in a capitalist system because such a system works toward the preservation of the wealth and power of those in charge and must necessarily exploit the working class to achieve this end.

2. *What do the vast stockyards, packed with animals, symbolize?*

The stockyards symbolize the plight of the common laborer, who is shuffled through the machinery of capitalism as a means to the end of corporate profit. Just as the stockyards are crammed with animals being herded to slaughter, so too are they packed with laborers systematically being destroyed by economic forces beyond their control. The factory owners have concern for the suffering of neither the animals nor the workers, viewing both as essential components of the meat-packing industry. In a sense, the laborers are nothing more than pieces of meat themselves—stripped of his identity, each laborer is merely a mass of muscles that, by helping the meat-packing plant run, factors into the general equation of consumption. Additionally, the crowded animal pens of the stockyards symbolize Packingtown's crowded living quarters for workers. With almost no personal space or privacy for the individual, Jurgis and his family are dehumanized by their accommodations. Similar to an animal, Jurgis exists, from a severe capitalist point of view, only to carry out his function at the meat-packing plant.

3. *How do Sinclair's political intentions affect the characters, style, and structure of the novel?*

In an effort to win converts to socialism, Sinclair constructs every formal element in as simple and transparent a way as possible. The narrative structure follows one long descent into the hellish reality of capitalism until Jurgis discovers socialism and is saved in a manner not unlike the evangelical Christian idea of being born again. Sinclair fleshes out this capitalist hell with a realistic style that relies heavily on stomach-churning description. Sinclair's realism falters with his characters, however. At times, they seem less like portraits of realistic people and more like one-dimensional representations of particular classes and social forces. While abstract forces such as capitalism and socialism do shape and sometimes suppress individual identities, one can argue that there is a tension between the flatness of Sinclair's characters and the human qualities with which he tries to instill them. Jurgis, for example, is called upon to represent an entire class of society *and* be a loving father, devoted husband, pitiful victim, and hero. He is asked to be a glorified abstraction *and* a particular person, but his role as representative of the proletariat seems to rob him of the real humanity that would make his struggle worthwhile. Along similar lines, the socialist characters exhibit a frightening degree of conformity and live with each other without antagonism or complexity. Their idealization runs seems somewhat at odds with the novel's claim, implicit in its style and setting, of being realistic.

How to Write Literary Analysis

The Literary Essay: A Step-by-Step Guide

When you read for pleasure, your only goal is enjoyment. You might find yourself reading to get caught up in an exciting story, to learn about an interesting time or place, or just to pass time. Maybe you're looking for inspiration, guidance, or a reflection of your own life. There are as many different, valid ways of reading a book as there are books in the world.

When you read a work of literature in an English class, however, you're being asked to read in a special way: you're being asked to perform *literary analysis*. To analyze something means to break it down into smaller parts and then examine how those parts work, both individually and together. Literary analysis involves examining all the parts of a novel, play, short story, or poem—elements such as character, setting, tone, and imagery—and thinking about how the author uses those elements to create certain effects.

A literary essay isn't a book review: you're not being asked whether or not you liked a book or whether you'd recommend it to another reader. A literary essay also isn't like the kind of book report you wrote when you were younger, where your teacher wanted you to summarize the book's action. A high school- or college-level literary essay asks, "How does this piece of literature actually work?" "How does it do what it does?" and, "Why might the author have made the choices he or she did?"

The Seven Steps

No one is born knowing how to analyze literature; it's a skill you learn and a process you can master. As you gain more practice with this kind of thinking and writing, you'll be able to craft a method that works best for you. But until then, here are seven basic steps to writing a well-constructed literary essay:

1. Ask questions
2. Collect evidence
3. Construct a thesis

4. Develop and organize arguments
5. Write the introduction
6. Write the body paragraphs
7. Write the conclusion

———

1. ASK QUESTIONS

When you're assigned a literary essay in class, your teacher will often provide you with a list of writing prompts. Lucky you! Now all you have to do is choose one. Do yourself a favor and pick a topic that interests you. You'll have a much better (not to mention easier) time if you start off with something you enjoy thinking about. If you are asked to come up with a topic by yourself, though, you might start to feel a little panicked. Maybe you have too many ideas—or none at all. Don't worry. Take a deep breath and start by asking yourself these questions:

- **What struck you?** Did a particular image, line, or scene linger in your mind for a long time? If it fascinated you, chances are you can draw on it to write a fascinating essay.

- **What confused you?** Maybe you were surprised to see a character act in a certain way, or maybe you didn't understand why the book ended the way it did. Confusing moments in a work of literature are like a loose thread in a sweater: if you pull on it, you can unravel the entire thing. Ask yourself why the author chose to write about that character or scene the way he or she did and you might tap into some important insights about the work as a whole.

- **Did you notice any patterns?** Is there a phrase that the main character uses constantly or an image that repeats throughout the book? If you can figure out how that pattern weaves through the work and what the significance of that pattern is, you've almost got your entire essay mapped out.

- **Did you notice any contradictions or ironies?** Great works of literature are complex; great literary essays recognize and explain those complexities. Maybe the title (*Happy Days*) totally disagrees with the book's subject matter (hungry orphans dying in the woods). Maybe the main character acts one way around his family and a completely different way around his friends and associates. If you can find a way to explain a work's contradictory elements, you've got the seeds of a great essay.

At this point, you don't need to know exactly what you're going to say about your topic; you just need a place to begin your exploration. You can help direct your reading and brainstorming by formulating your topic as a *question,* which you'll then try to answer in your essay. The best questions invite critical debates and discussions, not just a rehashing of the summary. Remember, you're looking for something you can *prove or argue* based on evidence you find in the text. Finally, remember to keep the scope of your question in mind: is this a topic you can adequately address within the word or page limit you've been given? Conversely, is this a topic big enough to fill the required length?

GOOD QUESTIONS

"Are Romeo and Juliet's parents responsible for the deaths of their children?"

"Why do pigs keep showing up in LORD OF THE FLIES?*"*
"Are Dr. Frankenstein and his monster alike? How?"

BAD QUESTIONS

"What happens to Scout in TO KILL A MOCKINGBIRD?*"*
"What do the other characters in JULIUS CAESAR *think about Caesar?"*
"How does Hester Prynne in THE SCARLET LETTER *remind me of my sister?"*

---

2. COLLECT EVIDENCE

Once you know what question you want to answer, it's time to scour the book for things that will help you answer the question. Don't worry if you don't know what you want to say yet—right now you're just collecting ideas and material and letting it all percolate. Keep track of passages, symbols, images, or scenes that deal with your topic. Eventually, you'll start making connections between these examples and your thesis will emerge.

Here's a brief summary of the various parts that compose each and every work of literature. These are the elements that you will analyze in your essay, and which you will offer as evidence to support your arguments. For more on the parts of literary works, see the Glossary of Literary Terms at the end of this section.

LITERARY ANALYSIS

ELEMENTS OF STORY   These are the *what*s of the work—what happens, where it happens, and to whom it happens.

- **Plot:** All of the events and actions of the work.
- **Character:** The people who act and are acted upon in a literary work. The main character of a work is known as the *protagonist*.
- **Conflict:** The central tension in the work. In most cases, the protagonist wants something, while opposing forces (antagonists) hinder the protagonist's progress.
- **Setting:** When and where the work takes place. Elements of setting include location, time period, time of day, weather, social atmosphere, and economic conditions.
- **Narrator:** The person telling the story. The narrator may straightforwardly report what happens, convey the subjective opinions and perceptions of one or more characters, or provide commentary and opinion in his or her own voice.
- **Themes:** The main idea or message of the work—usually an abstract idea about people, society, or life in general. A work may have many themes, which may be in tension with one another.

ELEMENTS OF STYLE   These are the *how*s—how the characters speak, how the story is constructed, and how language is used throughout the work.

- **Structure and organization:** How the parts of the work are assembled. Some novels are narrated in a linear, chronological fashion, while others skip around in time. Some plays follow a traditional three- or five-act structure, while others are a series of loosely connected scenes. Some authors deliberately leave gaps in their works, leaving readers to puzzle out the missing information. A work's structure and organization can tell you a lot about the kind of message it wants to convey.
- **Point of view:** The perspective from which a story is told. In *first-person point of view,* the narrator involves him or herself in the story. ("I went to the store"; "We watched in horror as the bird slammed into the window.") A first-person narrator is usually the protagonist of the work, but not always. In *third-person point of view,* the narrator does not participate

in the story. A third-person narrator may closely follow a specific character, recounting that individual character's thoughts or experiences, or it may be what we call an *omniscient* narrator. Omniscient narrators see and know all: they can witness any event in any time or place and are privy to the inner thoughts and feelings of all characters. Remember that the narrator and the author are not the same thing!

- **Diction:** Word choice. Whether a character uses dry, clinical language or flowery prose with lots of exclamation points can tell you a lot about his or her attitude and personality.

- **Syntax:** Word order and sentence construction. Syntax is a crucial part of establishing an author's narrative voice. Ernest Hemingway, for example, is known for writing in very short, straightforward sentences, while James Joyce characteristically wrote in long, incredibly complicated lines.

- **Tone:** The mood or feeling of the text. Diction and syntax often contribute to the tone of a work. A novel written in short, clipped sentences that use small, simple words might feel brusque, cold, or matter-of-fact.

- **Imagery:** Language that appeals to the senses, representing things that can be seen, smelled, heard, tasted, or touched.

- **Figurative language:** Language that is not meant to be interpreted literally. The most common types of figurative language are *metaphors* and *similes,* which compare two unlike things in order to suggest a similarity between them—for example, "All the world's a stage," or "The moon is like a ball of green cheese." (Metaphors say one thing *is* another thing; similes claim that one thing is *like* another thing.)

---

3. CONSTRUCT A THESIS

When you've examined all the evidence you've collected and know how you want to answer the question, it's time to write your thesis statement. A *thesis* is a claim about a work of literature that needs to be supported by evidence and arguments. The thesis statement is the heart of the literary essay, and the bulk of your paper will be spent trying to prove this claim. A good thesis will be:

- **Arguable.** "*The Great Gatsby* describes New York society in the 1920s" isn't a thesis—it's a fact.

- **Provable through textual evidence**. "*Hamlet* is a confusing but ultimately very well-written play" is a weak thesis because it offers the writer's personal opinion about the book. Yes, it's arguable, but it's not a claim that can be proved or supported with examples taken from the play itself.

- **Surprising**. "Both George and Lenny change a great deal in *Of Mice and Men*" is a weak thesis because it's obvious. A really strong thesis will argue for a reading of the text that is not immediately apparent.

- **Specific.** "Dr. Frankenstein's monster tells us a lot about the human condition" is *almost* a really great thesis statement, but it's still too vague. What does the writer mean by "a lot"? *How* does the monster tell us so much about the human condition?

GOOD THESIS STATEMENTS

Question: In *Romeo and Juliet*, which is more powerful in shaping the lovers' story: fate or foolishness?

Thesis: "Though Shakespeare defines Romeo and Juliet as 'star-crossed lovers' and images of stars and planets appear throughout the play, a closer examination of that celestial imagery reveals that the stars are merely witnesses to the characters' foolish activities and not the causes themselves."

Question: How does the bell jar function as a symbol in Sylvia Plath's *The Bell Jar*?

Thesis: "A bell jar is a bell-shaped glass that has three basic uses: to hold a specimen for observation, to contain gases, and to maintain a vacuum. The bell jar appears in each of these capacities in *The Bell Jar*, Plath's semi-autobiographical novel, and each appearances marks a different stage in Esther's mental breakdown."

Question: Would Piggy in *The Lord of the Flies* make a good island leader if he were given the chance?

Thesis: "Though the intelligent, rational, and innovative Piggy has the mental characteristics of a good leader, he ultimately lacks the social skills necessary to be an effective one. Golding emphasizes this point by giving Piggy a foil in the charismatic Jack, whose magnetic personality allows him to capture and wield power effectively, if not always wisely."

4. Develop and Organize Arguments

The reasons and examples that support your thesis will form the middle paragraphs of your essay. Since you can't really write your thesis statement until you know how you'll structure your argument, you'll probably end up working on steps 3 and 4 at the same time.

There's no single method of argumentation that will work in every context. One essay prompt might ask you to compare and contrast two characters, while another asks you to trace an image through a given work of literature. These questions require different kinds of answers and therefore different kinds of arguments. Below, we'll discuss three common kinds of essay prompts and some strategies for constructing a solid, well-argued case.

Types of Literary Essays

- **Compare and contrast**

  Compare and contrast the characters of Huck and Jim in The Adventures of Huckleberry Finn.

  Chances are you've written this kind of essay before. In an academic literary context, you'll organize your arguments the same way you would in any other class. You can either go *subject by subject* or *point by point*. In the former, you'll discuss one character first and then the second. In the latter, you'll choose several traits (attitude toward life, social status, images and metaphors associated with the character) and devote a paragraph to each. You may want to use a mix of these two approaches—for example, you may want to spend a paragraph a piece broadly sketching Huck's and Jim's personalities before transitioning into a paragraph or two that describes a few key points of comparison. This can be a highly effective strategy if you want to make a counterintuitive argument—that, despite seeming to be totally different, the two objects being compared are actually similar in a very important way (or vice versa). Remember that your essay should reveal something fresh or unexpected about the text, so think beyond the obvious parallels and differences.

- **Trace**

  Choose an image—for example, birds, knives, or eyes—and trace that image throughout Macbeth.

  Sounds pretty easy, right? All you need to do is read the play, underline every appearance of a knife in *Macbeth,* and then list them in your essay in the order they appear, right? Well, not exactly. Your teacher doesn't want a simple catalog of examples. He or she wants to see you make *connections* between those examples—that's the difference between summarizing and analyzing. In the *Macbeth* example above, think about the different contexts in which knives appear in the play and to what effect. In *Macbeth*, there are real knives and imagined knives; knives that kill and knives that simply threaten. Categorize and classify your examples to give them some order. Finally, always keep the overall effect in mind. After you choose and analyze your examples, you should come to some greater understanding about the work, as well as your chosen image, symbol, or phrase's role in developing the major themes and stylistic strategies of that work.

- **Debate**

    Is the society depicted in 1984 *good for its citizens?*

In this kind of essay, you're being asked to debate a moral, ethical, or aesthetic issue regarding the work. You might be asked to judge a character or group of characters (*Is Caesar responsible for his own demise?*) or the work itself (*Is* JANE EYRE *a feminist novel?*). For this kind of essay, there are two important points to keep in mind. First, don't simply base your arguments on your personal feelings and reactions. Every literary essay expects you to read and analyze the work, so search for evidence in the text. What do characters in 1984 have to say about the government of Oceania? What images does Orwell use that might give you a hint about his attitude toward the government? As in any debate, you also need to make sure that you define all the necessary terms before you begin to argue your case. What does it mean to be a "good" society? What makes a novel "feminist"? You should define your terms right up front, in the first paragraph after your introduction.

Second, remember that strong literary essays make contrary and surprising arguments. Try to think outside the box. In the 1984 example above, it seems like the obvious answer would be no, the totalitarian society depicted in Orwell's novel is *not* good for its citizens. But can you think of any arguments for the opposite side? Even if your final assertion is that the novel depicts a cruel, repressive, and therefore harmful society, acknowledging and responding to the counterargument will strengthen your overall case.

5. WRITE THE INTRODUCTION

Your introduction sets up the entire essay. It's where you present your topic and articulate the particular issues and questions you'll be addressing. It's also where you, as the writer, introduce yourself to your readers. A persuasive literary essay immediately establishes its writer as a knowledgeable, authoritative figure.

An introduction can vary in length depending on the overall length of the essay, but in a traditional five-paragraph essay it should be no longer than one paragraph. However long it is, your introduction needs to:

- **Provide any necessary context.** Your introduction should situate the reader and let him or her know what to expect. What book are you discussing? Which characters? What topic will you be addressing?

- **Answer the "So what?" question.** Why is this topic important, and why is your particular position on the topic noteworthy? Ideally, your introduction should pique the reader's interest by suggesting how your argument is surprising or otherwise counterintuitive. Literary essays make unexpected connections and reveal less-than-obvious truths.

- **Present your thesis.** This usually happens at or very near the end of your introduction.

- **Indicate the shape of the essay to come.** Your reader should finish reading your introduction with a good sense of the scope of your essay as well as the path you'll take toward proving your thesis. You don't need to spell out every step, but you do need to suggest the organizational pattern you'll be using.

Your introduction should not:

- **Be vague.** Beware of the two killer words in literary analysis: *interesting* and *important*. Of course the work, question, or example is interesting and important—that's why you're writing about it!

- **Open with any grandiose assertions.** Many student readers think that beginning their essays with a flamboyant statement such as, "Since the dawn of time, writers have been fascinated with the topic of free will," makes them sound important and commanding. You know what? It actually sounds pretty amateurish.

- **Wildly praise the work.** Another typical mistake student writers make is extolling the work or author. Your teacher doesn't need to be told that "Shakespeare is perhaps the greatest writer in the English language." You can mention a work's reputation in passing—by referring to *The Adventures of Huckleberry Finn* as "Mark Twain's enduring classic," for example—but don't make a point of bringing it up unless that reputation is key to your argument.

- **Go off-topic.** Keep your introduction streamlined and to the point. Don't feel the need to throw in all kinds of bells and whistles in order to impress your reader—just get to the point as quickly as you can, without skimping on any of the required steps.

---

6. WRITE THE BODY PARAGRAPHS

Once you've written your introduction, you'll take the arguments you developed in step 4 and turn them into your body paragraphs. The organization of this middle section of your essay will largely be determined by the argumentative strategy you use, but no matter how you arrange your thoughts, your body paragraphs need to do the following:

- **Begin with a strong topic sentence.** Topic sentences are like signs on a highway: they tell the reader where they are and where they're going. A good topic sentence not only alerts readers to what issue will be discussed in the following paragraph but also gives them a sense of what argument will be made *about* that issue. "Rumor and gossip play an important role in *The Crucible*" isn't a strong topic sentence because it doesn't tell us very much. "The community's constant gossiping creates an environment that allows false accusations to flourish" is a much stronger topic sentence— it not only tells us *what* the paragraph will discuss (gossip) but *how* the paragraph will discuss the topic (by showing how gossip creates a set of conditions that leads to the play's climactic action).

- **Fully and completely develop a single thought.** Don't skip around in your paragraph or try to stuff in too much material. Body paragraphs are like bricks: each individual

THE JUNGLE ❧ 77

one needs to be strong and sturdy or the entire structure will collapse. Make sure you have really proven your point before moving on to the next one.

- **Use transitions effectively.** Good literary essay writers know that each paragraph must be clearly and strongly linked to the material around it. Think of each paragraph as a response to the one that precedes it. Use transition words and phrases such as *however, similarly, on the contrary, therefore,* and *furthermore* to indicate what kind of response you're making.

---

7. WRITE THE CONCLUSION

Just as you used the introduction to ground your readers in the topic before providing your thesis, you'll use the conclusion to quickly summarize the specifics learned thus far and then hint at the broader implications of your topic. A good conclusion will:

- **Do more than simply restate the thesis.** If your thesis argued that *The Catcher in the Rye* can be read as a Christian allegory, don't simply end your essay by saying, "And that is why *The Catcher in the Rye* can be read as a Christian allegory." If you've constructed your arguments well, this kind of statement will just be redundant.

- **Synthesize the arguments, not summarize them.** Similarly, don't repeat the details of your body paragraphs in your conclusion. The reader has already read your essay, and chances are it's not so long that they've forgotten all your points by now.

- **Revisit the "So what?" question.** In your introduction, you made a case for why your topic and position are important. You should close your essay with the same sort of gesture. What do your readers know now that they didn't know before? How will that knowledge help them better appreciate or understand the work overall?

- **Move from the specific to the general.** Your essay has most likely treated a very specific element of the work—a single character, a small set of images, or a particular passage. In your conclusion, try to show how this narrow discussion has wider implications for the work overall. If your essay on *To Kill a Mockingbird* focused on the character of Boo Radley, for example, you might want to include a bit in your

LITERARY ANALYSIS

conclusion about how he fits into the novel's larger message about childhood, innocence, or family life.

- **Stay relevant.** Your conclusion should suggest new directions of thought, but it shouldn't be treated as an opportunity to pad your essay with all the extra, interesting ideas you came up with during your brainstorming sessions but couldn't fit into the essay proper. Don't attempt to stuff in unrelated queries or too many abstract thoughts.

- **Avoid making overblown closing statements.** A conclusion should open up your highly specific, focused discussion, but it should do so without drawing a sweeping lesson about life or human nature. Making such observations may be part of the point of reading, but it's almost always a mistake in essays, where these observations tend to sound overly dramatic or simply silly.

A+ ESSAY CHECKLIST

Congratulations! If you've followed all the steps we've outlined above, you should have a solid literary essay to show for all your efforts. What if you've got your sights set on an A+? To write the kind of superlative essay that will be rewarded with a perfect grade, keep the following rubric in mind. These are the qualities that teachers expect to see in a truly A+ essay. How does yours stack up?

- ✓ Demonstrates a thorough understanding of the book
- ✓ Presents an original, compelling argument
- ✓ Thoughtfully analyzes the text's formal elements
- ✓ Uses appropriate and insightful examples
- ✓ Structures ideas in a logical and progressive order
- ✓ Demonstrates a mastery of sentence construction, transitions, grammar, spelling, and word choice

LITERARY ANALYSIS

Suggested Essay Topics

1. *How does the title of* THE JUNGLE *relate to the themes of the novel? Give specific examples.*

2. *In what ways does Sinclair depict capitalism as destructive? Consider the characters' personal lives and social interactions.*

3. *Do you find Sinclair's argument for socialism persuasive? Why or why not? How does Sinclair try to persuade the reading public to accept socialism?*

A+ STUDENT ESSAY

> Upton Sinclair famously remarked about *The Jungle:* "I aimed at the public's heart and by accident I hit it in the stomach." If Sinclair's aim was to arouse a sympathetic response, why does the novel fail to perform its intended function?

In *The Jungle,* his exposé of immigrant labor, Upton Sinclair had two seemingly compatible goals: to stimulate outrage at the practice of selling diseased meat to the public and to arouse sympathy for laborers who worked in the unsanitary conditions of the warehouses. However, in his novel, Sinclair places psychologically shallow, unrealistic characters in an extremely detailed, realistic environment, causing readers to be more affected by Packingtown's horrific conditions than by the emotional and psychological damage inflicted on its residents. The novel sabotages Sinclair's second intention by forcing readers to see, smell, and taste the environment of the meatpacking industry while simultaneously preventing them from sympathizing with the workers who endure its inhumane conditions.

Though *The Jungle* is a work of fiction, Sinclair's use of highly evocative details and imagery links the novel to a type of journalism called "muckraking," which was at its height in the years between the 1890s and 1920s. Muckraking journalists aimed to expose social misconduct through explicit descriptions of shocking conditions and actions, but these writers were rarely interested in nuanced behavioral analysis. Sinclair's journalistic style of writing registers with photographic precision the external conditions in which the immigrants work. The novel bursts with the gritty, visceral details of Packingtown, and at times it seems as if Sinclair is describing a deserted battlefield rather than a production zone for consumer goods: Packingtown is full of rivers of blood and rotting carcasses. Sinclair emphasized the filthy conditions of the warehouses in the hopes that the revolting depictions would cause the reading public to press for the reform of the immigrants' working conditions. The public, though, proved more affected by sensation than by sympathy. Indeed, Sinclair's descriptive reportage clearly aims at "the stomach"; the novel lingers on gory images of poisoned rats and rusty nails in breakfast sausages. As the reading public's response to *The Jungle* would seem to indicate, Sinclair's dedication to blunt and sensational detail was useful for depicting the laborers' external circumstances, but not their internal anguish or psychological conflict.

The graphic realism of the Packingtown environment engages readers through the stimulation of their senses, but in order to understand the human costs of such unsafe and unsanitary working conditions readers need to feel a sympathetic connection to the workers. In order to accomplish his second goal—prompting reforms to help protect laborers—Sinclair needed to create characters that the upper- and middle-class readers of *The Jungle* could identify with. However, in his attempt to make his protagonist, Jurgis, sympathetic, Sinclair ends up idealizing him. Patriotic, hardworking, and a devoted son and new husband, the young Lithuanian immigrant is free from any personal flaws. Any adverse consequence seems to occur through no fault of his own, but rather because of environmental contingencies. For example, Sinclair emphasizes how capitalism causes Jurgis's descent into alcoholism, his abandonment of his family, and his falling prey to the influence of reprobates. He makes this clear by showing how Jurgis's discovery of Socialist politics restores the humanity that capitalism had taken away from him. After attending the socialist meetings, for example, Jurgis returns immediately to work and to his family, instantly rehabilitated by the other "comrades." Moreover, by overemphasizing his goodness in the face of the industry barons' corruption, Sinclair portrays Jurgis as a wholly passive victim rather than an active agent. Such idealism results in a flat, static character, devoid of any realistic humanity. Ironically, the fact that Jurgis has no unsympathetic traits makes it difficult for readers to identify with him. It is no surprise, then, that Sinclair's initial readers would feel more drawn into the visceral world of Packingtown—a world that engages them on the levels of sight, smell, sound, taste, and touch—and less concerned with characters that hardly seem like real people at all.

The fact that *The Jungle* featured an unsympathetic protagonist and unbelievable characters didn't deter the reading public, who turned the book into a bestseller and whose outcry against the meat packing industry's low standards resulted in the 1906 Pure Food and Drug Act. If the public still persisted in advocating for a law that would protect them from consuming potentially tainted meat products, even when faced with the doubtful realism of key aspects of the novel, such as its characters, it paradoxically proves Sinclair's fundamental point: Human individuals are nothing if not self-interested.

GLOSSARY OF LITERARY TERMS

ANTAGONIST

> The entity that acts to frustrate the goals of the *protagonist*. The antagonist is usually another *character* but may also be a non-human force.

ANTIHERO / ANTIHEROINE

> A *protagonist* who is not admirable or who challenges notions of what should be considered admirable.

CHARACTER

> A person, animal, or any other thing with a personality that appears in a *narrative*.

CLIMAX

> The moment of greatest intensity in a text or the major turning point in the *plot*.

CONFLICT

> The central struggle that moves the *plot* forward. The conflict can be the *protagonist*'s struggle against fate, nature, society, or another person.

FIRST-PERSON POINT OF VIEW

> A literary style in which the *narrator* tells the story from his or her own *point of view* and refers to himself or herself as "I." The narrator may be an active participant in the story or just an observer.

HERO / HEROINE

> The principal *character* in a literary work or *narrative*.

IMAGERY

> Language that brings to mind sense-impressions, representing things that can be seen, smelled, heard, tasted, or touched.

MOTIF

> A recurring idea, structure, contrast, or device that develops or informs the major *themes* of a work of literature.

NARRATIVE

> A story.

NARRATOR

The person (sometimes a *character*) who tells a story; the *voice* assumed by the writer. The narrator and the author of the work of literature are not the same person.

PLOT

The arrangement of the events in a story, including the sequence in which they are told, the relative emphasis they are given, and the causal connections between events.

POINT OF VIEW

The *perspective* that a *narrative* takes toward the events it describes.

PROTAGONIST

The main *character* around whom the story revolves.

SETTING

The location of a *narrative* in time and space. Setting creates mood or atmosphere.

SUBPLOT

A secondary *plot* that is of less importance to the overall story but may serve as a point of contrast or comparison to the main plot.

SYMBOL

An object, *character,* figure, or color that is used to represent an abstract idea or concept. Unlike an *emblem,* a symbol may have different meanings in different contexts.

SYNTAX

The way the words in a piece of writing are put together to form lines, phrases, or clauses; the basic structure of a piece of writing.

THEME

A fundamental and universal idea explored in a literary work.

TONE

The author's attitude toward the subject or *characters* of a story or poem or toward the reader.

VOICE

An author's individual way of using language to reflect his or her own personality and attitudes. An author communicates voice through *tone, diction,* and *syntax.*

LITERARY ANALYSIS

A NOTE ON PLAGIARISM

Plagiarism—presenting someone else's work as your own—rears its ugly head in many forms. Many students know that copying text without citing it is unacceptable. But some don't realize that even if you're not quoting directly, but instead are paraphrasing or summarizing, *it is plagiarism* unless you cite the source.

Here are the most common forms of plagiarism:

- Using an author's phrases, sentences, or paragraphs without citing the source
- Paraphrasing an author's ideas without citing the source
- Passing off another student's work as your own

How do you steer clear of plagiarism? You should *always* acknowledge all words and ideas that aren't your own by using quotation marks around verbatim text or citations like footnotes and endnotes to note another writer's ideas. For more information on how to give credit when credit is due, ask your teacher for guidance or visit www.sparknotes.com.

LITERARY ANALYSIS

Review & Resources

Quiz

1. Who is the first person to abandon the family?

    A. Jonas
    B. Jurgis
    C. Marija
    D. Ona

2. Who develops a drug addiction?

    A. Ona
    B. Jokubas
    C. Marija
    D. Elzbieta

3. Why is Jurgis sent to prison the first time?

    A. For public drunkenness
    B. For attacking Phil Connor
    C. For raping Ona
    D. For destroying the farmer's peach trees

4. Who plays the violin?

    A. Tamoszius
    B. Jurgis
    C. Ona
    D. Jokubas

5. Whose delicatessen is a financial failure?

    A. Tamoszius
    B. Jurgis
    C. Ona
    D. Jokubas

6. Why is Stanislovas afraid of the cold on winter mornings?

    A. Because he hates slipping on the ice
    B. Because he has seen the effects of frostbite
    C. Because he has to work outdoors
    D. Because he only earns money on warm days

7. Where is Ostrinski from?

    A. Lithuania
    B. Russia
    C. Romania
    D. Poland

8. In what year was *The Jungle* first published?

    A. 1906
    B. 1912
    C. 1911
    D. 1910

9. What law was passed due to public outcry caused by the novel?

    A. The Food and Drug Reform Bill
    B. The Countermeasure
    C. The Pure Food and Drug Act of 1906
    D. The Wage Reform Standards Act

10. How does the young Antanas die?

    A. He is killed by a steer.
    B. He drowns in the mud-logged street.
    C. He eats bad sausage.
    D. He catches frostbite.

11. At the beginning of the novel, what is Jurgis's response to learning of the debt caused by his marriage feast?

    A. "I will earn more."
    B. "I will try harder."
    C. "I will work more."
    D. "I will work harder."

12. How does Kristoforas die?

    A. He eats diseased meat.

    B. He drowns in the mud-logged street.

    C. He is killed by an angry union member to punish Jurgis for breaking the strike.

    D. He falls off of a carriage.

13. From what country do Jurgis and Ona emigrate?

    A. Poland

    B. Iceland

    C. Lithuania

    D. Croatia

14. To what political party does Mike Scully belong?

    A. The Republicans

    B. The Democrats

    C. The Socialists

    D. The Communists

15. What is Teta Elzbieta's relationship to Ona?

    A. Elzbieta is Ona's mother.

    B. Elzbieta is Ona's aunt.

    C. Elzbieta is Ona's daughter.

    D. Elzbieta is Ona's stepmother.

16. Who becomes a prostitute?

    A. Ona

    B. Marija

    C. Jurgis

    D. Elzbieta

17. What does Jurgis seek to avenge in attacking Connor?

    A. Connor's murder of Stanislovas

    B. Connor's rape of Marija

    C. Connor's rape of Ona

    D. Connor's firing of Marija

18. Where does the philanthropic woman find a job for Jurgis?

    A. At a steel mill
    B. At a fertilizer plant
    C. On the killing beds
    D. In a bratwurst factory

19. To what political party does Tommy Hinds belong?

    A. The Republicans
    B. The Democrats
    C. The Socialists
    D. The Communists

20. Who convinces Jurgis to live for Antanas after Ona's death?

    A. Marija
    B. Teta Elzbieta
    C. Dede Antanas
    D. Kristoforas

21. What does Freddie Jones give to Jurgis?

    A. A rabbit's foot
    B. A car
    C. A one-hundred-dollar bill
    D. A gold watch

22. Why does Jack Duane leave town?

    A. Because his associates abandon him after he barely escapes arrest
    B. Because he longs to see the Pacific Ocean
    C. Because his wife and children have died
    D. Because he has heard that there are higher wages in Lithuania

23. Why do Marija and Tamoszius postpone their marriage?

    A. Because they are unsure about their feelings for each other
    B. Because Marija no longer loves Tamoszius
    C. Because Tamoszius no longer loves Marija
    D. Because they cannot afford to get married